CLAY

Memoirs of a Gardening Man

CLAY

Memoirs of a Gardening Man

CLAY JONES

CHAPMANS

Chapmans Publishers
A division of the Orion Publishing Group Ltd
Orion House
5 Upper St Martin's Lane
London WC2H 9EA

A CIP catalogue record for this book is available from the
British Library

ISBN 1 85592 569 9

First published by Chapmans 1993

Filmset by Selwood Systems, Midsomer Norton, Avon.

Printed in Great Britain by
Butler & Tanner Ltd, Frome and London

To Glen
my wife, my life, my all

Contents

૪૭

Moulding Clay

IT was the eighth of November 1923. The town of Cardigan
on the West Wales coast throbbed with subdued excitement. Strong men spoke in hushed tones, womenfolk gathered in small groups on street corners to chatter, yet forgot
to gossip, and wide-eyed children scuttled to and fro with
astonishing vigour. Into this world of teeming tension Annie
Margaret Clay-Jones gave birth to her first-born – me. In actual
fact, my coming passed unnoticed except by a smattering of
aunts, uncles and cousins who were, I'm told, mildly pleased
that a son had been born to fortify the ranks of Clays and
Joneses. The heightened beat of the town's pulse was all due
to the Annual Fair that was scheduled to transform normally
sedate and quiet Cardigan into a hive of noisy activity on the
tenth day of that month. For the first time in her young life,
my mother missed the Fair and to her dying day, I believe, she
held me responsible for confining her to bed when, all around
her, people were making whoopee. To make matters worse,
we lived not a hundred yards from the fairground, and from
her bed she could hear the piped music and the revelry. Of
course, I was oblivious to it all, but in the early evening of the
eighth, an event occurred which has influenced my days ever
since. Shortly after six o'clock, Mother developed an uncontrollable craving for fish and chips. One of the attendant aunts
was despatched hotfoot to the shop of Wilson the Fish and, on
her return, Mother demolished the lot with relish, so I was
told. Shortly afterwards I decided that I was ill-equipped to
compete for space with sixpenn'orth of cod and chips, and I

1

left. I swear that the prenatal meal accounts for the fact that I suffer withdrawal symptoms, even now, if I am denied my fish and chips for any length of time.

Before going any further with my life history, I must, once and for all time, dispel the belief that my surname is contrived. There are those among us who are convinced that the Clay bit was tagged on to the Jones bit later in life, when I decided that it was a gardener's life for me. It was not so. It happened thus – prior to her marriage, Mother was a Miss Clay, the only daughter of a Pembrokeshire farming family. Father was William Jones, born and bred in Cardigan and one of five children, four sons and a daughter. His father plied his trade as a ship's blacksmith in the days when the town was a thriving port and ship-building was of paramount importance to its prosperity. The eldest of father's brothers lost his life at sea during the Great War of 1914–1918; the youngest brother never married and, although both the other brother and sister were espoused, neither bore fruit. Mother had two brothers, both married, one remained childless and the other sired a daughter late in life. So it was that my grandmother, Elizabeth Clay, foresaw the day when the Clay dynasty could become defunct, unless her daughter's son perpetuated the name, and I was duly Christened Clay-Jones.

To return to my early childhood – we lived in a three-storey, rather rambling house, as near as dammit to the town centre. 'We' comprised Mother, Grandmother and me and – for short periods with long absences in between – my father. He was a marine engineer in the Merchant Navy and spent more of his life at sea than he did on land. In those early days I hardly knew him but, as his infrequent homecomings were always accompanied by gifts, I soon learnt to anticipate his appearance with great pleasure. Although communications in those bygone days were primitive compared to today, Mother followed Dad's marine progress via the shipping reports in the South Wales newspaper, the *Western Mail*. For example, we would read 'the SS *Llanfair* left Haifa bound for Cardiff', followed by the date. Later the ship would be reported as 'off

Gibraltar' and then she knew, almost to the day, when we could expect Dad to arrive home. He was the nicest and gentlest of any man I've ever known and I still deeply regret that I saw so little of him during my formative years.

Despite my father's frequent and prolonged absences, we three – Grandma, Mam and I – constituted a happy household. Grandmother was one of the most self-willed and self-possessed people that ever trod this earth, otherwise she would never have survived a series of traumatic experiences in her married life. She often confided in me, and I learnt that she had fallen in love and married William Clay at an early age. He was the son of a Fishguard sea captain, the proud owner of his own ship under sail, who traded between his home port and ports around the coasts of Britain and the Mediterranean. Her own family, the Perkinses, had not approved of the marriage, considering that she had 'married beneath her', as the saying goes, so they had bought the young newly-weds a 400-acre farm and, apparently, left them to it. Sadly Grandmother's first child, a boy, died when he was but a year old and when she spoke of 'little Thomas', even decades later, her face softened and here eyes welled with tears. Infant mortality was commonplace in the nineteenth century, but none the less tragic. She bore four more children and one of those died at childbirth. Her day of deepest darkness was still to come, for at the age of thirty-two her husband disappeared at sea. On his last voyage he set sail from Fishguard and neither he nor his crew were ever seen again. According to my grandmother, it was presumed that the ship went down with all hands in a fierce storm in the notorious Bay of Biscay. She was left to tend three young children and the farm. For years she fought the land and won. Her eldest surviving son was trained and qualified as a marine engineer; she set up her other son, the youngest child, in business as an auctioneer and then, and only then, did she give up the struggle and sell the farm. At that time both boys were serving their apprenticeships in Cardigan, so Grandma and my mother bought a house in the town and completely changed the course of their lives. A measure of my

3

grandmother's steel is that she outlived her husband by sixty years, eventually passing peacefully on at the age of ninety-two with all her faculties intact.

Until comparatively recently, Cardigan depended on the sea for its very existence, and it was the sea that accounts for my own arrival. In those days, around the turn of the century, nearly every able-bodied, able-brained son went to The Foundry. This was an establishment on the banks of the River Tivy that provided training for young men in the innards, maintenance and repair of marine engines. It was owned and managed by a man whom everyone knew as Matthew Bach (Little Matthew), who, presumably, was of small stature, or possibly a lovable character, since the Welsh word *bach* can mean either 'little' or 'endearing'. Anyway, he turned out a succession of highly-qualified marine engineers and it was said that a Matthew Bach engineer was on board every ship that sailed the seven seas. It was in The Foundry that my father met Morris, my mother's brother. They became firm friends. Father was invited home for tea and buns, met my mother, fell for her hook, line and anchor, married her and eventually I arrived on the scene. In retrospect, it was the germination of Clay-Jones, the gardener, all those years ago.

By the age of five I had learned a lesson that has stood me in good stead, and experienced my first taste of fear. The lesson was taught on a Monday morning when I was a mere two or possibly three years old. Monday was washing day, by tradition. Washing machines and spin-dryers were things of the future and our 'machine' consisted of a large cast-iron cauldron built into a brick surround, complete with a miniature furnace below and a tall chimney above, all housed in a custom-built wash-house. The fire was lit before breakfast, the cauldron filled with cold water carried from the kitchen tap, and by nine o'clock the great wash was underway and I was in my element. I had been given a small wooden wheelbarrow which I trundled to and fro, carrying wood to fuel the fire. I was important, at least I thought so, but I got careless. On this Monday morning, Mother had left a zinc bath full of dirty water outside the wash-house door and, as I reversed my barrow, I fell into it. I cried my eyes out; so did mother – with laughter. As she hauled her dripping, despondent offspring out of the murky depths she said, 'There, that'll teach you to look where you're going.' How true. I've never forgotten her words. They taught me to anticipate my progress both physically and metaphorically and they have saved me from unwise, precipitate action on many occasions. My second taste of fear I shall come to later.

The wash-house was built on to a section of the gable end of the main house and projected some way into a rather typical Victorian-style long and narrow back garden. A path ran down the centre, with fruit trees and bushes on one side and a vegetable garden on the other. Being country born and bred, the small plot of earth was a poor substitute for the 400 acres Mother had left behind in Pembrokeshire. Still, it was better than nothing and she made good use of every foot of soil and grew a succession of delicious vegetables. The first signs of intensive gardening activity occurred in late winter/early spring, when a horse and cart drew up in the lane at the back garden gate and off-loaded a huge pile of rich, aromatic cow manure. The provider of this bounty was Dafi Laca (or rather his cows), who ran a small dairy farm within 300 yards of the town centre and supplied most of Cardigan's households with fresh, untested, beautiful milk. His odd name, Dafi Laca, stems from the peculiarly Welsh habit of investing people with nicknames, or of adding the name of the farm, the house, or a trade to the surname. Thus Evan Griffiths of Penlan Farm was known as Griffiths Penlan, and an uncle of mine who was a coal merchant was Jones the Coal. Dafi Laca's nickname also reflected Cardigan's seafaring history. His Christian name was Dafydd or David and, as *laca* is a foreign word for milk, the town's mariners picked up the word in some far-off port and bestowed it on Dafi.

The influence of foreign lands is still evident in Cardigan to this day. Walk the streets and you will find houses with such improbable names as 'Umsinga', 'Rosario', and others that are strange-sounding in a small Welsh town which, until the Second World War, was predominantly Welsh-speaking ... although that is not strictly true either. The seafarers spent the greater part of their lives speaking in English to their fellows and to a motley crew of Lascars, Greeks, Arabs and others whose English was often rather ragged. In consequence, the Welsh mariners themselves developed a tongue that was neither wholly Welsh nor English. I recall a thoroughly Welsh sea captain being interviewed on television and making this hybrid announcement: *'Rown i'n gweld y ship yn disappearo yn y mist'*, meaning, 'I could see the ship disappearing in the mist.' The captains were not immune to being accorded nicknames. Many were humorous and ingenuous, as was that bestowed on an ancient mariner who had long lost his sea-legs and all his teeth – with the exception of one prominent incisor, smack in the centre of his mouth. Not surprisingly, he was dubbed, 'Sam Central-Eating'.

I knew fear for the second time in my life in Cardiff, which was my father's home port. Having sailed the oceans and dropped anchor in foreign lands, sometimes for several months, Dad and his ship would eventually make landfall in a British port but, although the ship was berthed for unloading, it could not be left unattended; a duty engineer had to be present at all times. Depending on the size and tonnage of the vessel, the ship's crew could comprise four or five engineers and they took it in turns to man the engine-room in port. So there were times when my father had to remain on board. It was only natural that, as Father couldn't come home to Mother, she packed her bags and went to him, and I was the extra baggage. Normally, both Mother and I were permitted to stay aboard ship, sharing Dad's cabin, but on this one occasion, in Cardiff, we couldn't for some reason. So we went into digs near the docks, in a long street of terraced houses that were all identical, like peas in a pod. At the far end of the street stood a veritable Aladdin's cave – a shop that sold sweets, pop and all the other goodies that drew a four-year-old lad like a magnet. There was a problem – Mam knew that I could find my way to the temple of temptation with ease, but could I find my way back and locate the right house among so many that looked exactly alike? She solved the dilemma by placing a picture postcard of a furry pussy-cat in the bay window. It worked a treat and I homed in on it on my initial safari. Then disaster struck – the wind or something dislodged the pictured pussy-cat and I was a lost soul in alien surroundings. I did what any child would do in the circumstances – I panicked. I stood in the street and howled my head off. I was soon surrounded by a bevy of solicitous ladies and restored intact, but all of a tremble, into the arms of my mother. I have felt fear many times since, but those moments of terrible terror are etched in my memory for all time.

Memories of early childhood are fleeting, and those that are permanently recorded, are few and significant. They are stamped on the memory cells, because they recall either emotional crises or events that gave great pleasure. Although not yet five years old at the time, I can remember a holiday that was the fulfilment of every childhood dream. Father's ship had docked in the port of Avonmouth and it fell to his lot to act as duty officer on board. Once again, Mother packed me and her bags and, with breathless excitement on my part, we boarded the train in Cardigan station and set out for Bristol. Stage one of the journey took us to the junction at Whitland, where it was all change for stage two on to the main-line train from Fishguard to London with, among others, a stop at Cardiff to off-load Mrs Jones and her offspring to board yet another train for the final stage of the journey to Bristol. Stages two and three in the Great Western Railway's yellow and brown carriages drawn by great, coal-fired engines were rapid; stage one was not. The Cardigan-to-Whitland train took its time, stopping at every one-man station *en route* to collect a possible passenger, but more likely to pick up churns of milk and wicker baskets of rabbit carcasses, destined for some town or city market. The engine driver knew everyone along the route and was known to halt the train in the middle of nowhere to deliver a letter or parcel to a remote farmstead. It was a standing joke that on one occasion the train came upon a man walking up the line and on being offered a lift, he declined, saying he was in a hurry to get to his destination. They were unhurried times, long before rats raced, when a day was long enough and people paced their lives according to their modest means and desires.

So eventually Mother and I arrived in Bristol, where we were met by Father and conveyed the last few miles to the ship in Avonmouth docks. The cabin was too small to accommodate all three of us, so I was allocated an adjoining cabin, normally the preserve of the Third engineer, who had gone home on leave. I thereupon became the Third engineer in all but reality, and went about the ship trying my very best to muster an air of authority. The seamen still on board were Lascars and Greeks, and they readily pandered to my whims by saluting and addressing me as 'Chief'. I was proud of my new-found rank and station and even more so when I was allowed to wear my father's peaked hat and badge. It was several sizes too big but, packed with several sheets of newspaper, it stayed perched on my head. As in Cardiff, there was another source of sweets and pop in Avonmouth. The shop was a short distance outside the dock gates and every morning I was despatched to collect the daily milk, papers and other bits and pieces. Resplendent in Father's hat, I passed through the dock gates where the duty policeman came smartly to attention and saluted, a process that was repeated on my return, a few minutes later. We sojourned on ship for a whole month and, when the time came for departure, I had attained the rank of Admiral!

Today things would be very different. The shop has long since been superseded by a supermarket, I suppose, and I would not be allowed to make the daily journey on my own, as my safety would be at risk. All those years ago, in the late twenties, children walked free and our parents were never troubled by the thought that we might come to any harm that was not of our own making. They were happy days and my memory of that Avonmouth holiday is one of an endless succession of blue skies and sunny days, unbroken by real or imaginary clouds. The ship was unloading grain, sucked up from its cavernous holds by a vast metal tube that deposited its intake into railway trucks, parked on the quayside. I stood for hours, watching the grain being remorselessly gulped by the metal monster, but the best was yet to come. When the holds were empty, they were ready to receive their next cargo – coal, and where there's coal, there's coal-dust. For some reason, small boys and dust have an affinity, the one for the other, and I was no exception. In the summer warmth, I was clad in a pair of shorts and nothing else and, by the time loading ceased for the day, I was blissfully happy and as black as an undertaker. Mother didn't seem to mind – she'd had the day to herself – and my blackened body was de-coaled in a large tub of water with the help of a tablet of Lifebuoy soap.

I remember great excitement one morning. Mother and I were together in Dad's cabin when the door burst open, Father dashed in, grabbed us both by the hand and swept us out on deck. He pointed to the blue sky and there was a silver cigar glistening in the sunshine and moving slowly across the heavens. It was the airship R 101, a sight I shall never forget.

Back at home life returned to normal, but briefly. I contracted double pneumonia, a common enough disease in those days and one that often proved fatal. Today's antibiotics were unknown and so for several days I hovered precariously between life and death. I was told later that even the doctor had despaired of my recovery, but I confounded them all and returned to the land of the living from the depths of unconsciousness, and I remember that moment well. I opened my eyes to a darkened bedroom, lit only by a candle flickering on the mantelpiece. The room was empty and, once I'd come to terms with my situation, I realised that I was ravenously hungry. I could not have taken any sustenance for some time and, now that the germ warfare had subsided, my fragile frame demanded food. Summoning all my resources, I called for attention and both Grandmother and Mother came belting up the stairs. The look of relief on their faces spoke volumes, and when I told them I was hungry their joy knew no bounds. I was asked what I would like and, to their astonishment, I opted for a plateful of fried tomatoes. At that very moment the doctor arrived, probably carrying a death certificate in his bag, just in case! My odd request was revealed and his words were, 'give him anything he fancies'. In no time at all, a platter of fried tomatoes accompanied by thin slices of bread and butter were before me, and all were devoured before you could say 'Moneymaker'. I've enjoyed many a memorable meal in my time, but none have compared with the repast that began my road to recovery. I still pay homage to and grow my favourite fruit – the tomato or Love Apple as it was once called. When it first came to Britain, the tomato was grown purely as an ornamental plant and only became universally popular when it was claimed to possess aphrodisiac properties, hence, Love Apple. I've eaten hundredweights of the rich red fruits over the years and, well, I'm not complaining.

My joust with double pneumonia left me with a persistent hacking cough. Dr Davies prescribed a variety of medicines which I dutifully swallowed, all to no avail. The cough got worse, until finally Grandmother took matters into her own hands. She knew and had great faith in a herbalist in Fishguard, and so to Fishguard by bus we went, Grandma, Mam and I. We arrived at a terraced house overlooking the harbour. A lady ushered us into a small front room, so crowded with furniture and bric à brac that it resembled an antique shop. Within minutes, a small man entered, passed the time of day with Grandmother and then sat me in a hard, high-backed chair facing the lace-curtained window. He placed himself in front and a little to one side of me and gazed raptly at me for what seemed several minutes. His were the most piercing eyes I've ever seen. They seemed to penetrate to the bone marrow and I felt that he could read my innermost thoughts, which at that moment were, 'What a funny fellow he is.' At last he broke the unbearable silence and, speaking to no one in particular, he announced in a loud, confident voice, 'The boy's got TB.' Not knowing what TB was, I remained unmoved, but my kith and kin were visibly shaken. The little man left the room and returned bearing quite a large brown paper bag containing a concoction of herbs, and ordered that I should be dosed with a teaspoonful of the stuff every day until all had been consumed. Mam and Grandma saw to it that I complied with the instructions and, although the mixture tasted like unripe compost, I took it and was cured. Every Friday evening I was also dosed with either Syrup of Figs, or Senna Pods tea, to 'keep my bowels open'. The amalgam of all three vile-tasting draughts was instrumental in my metamorphosis from a rather puny child into a comparatively robust stripling.

Living in Cardigan town in the twenties and early thirties had much to commend it. With most of the menfolk at sea, it was a matriarchal society. The women ruled the roost with a rod of iron, tempered with kindness and understanding. Besides Grandma and Mam, I had a clutch of aunts strategically placed around the town. There were aunties Rosa, Lea, Millie, Sal, Nurse, White-Jones and an 'auntie *drws nesa*' (auntie 'next door') who wasn't even distantly related, but merited the title because she plied me with good things. On Saturday mornings I did the rounds. Being the only male offspring, I was the apple of many eyes and usually picked up sufficient coinage to keep me in sweets for the rest of the week. But there was much more to it than that. Subconsciously, I was cocooned in a web of love and security and protected, perhaps over-protected, from the harsh realities of life. Tended hand and foot at home by two doting women and further idolised by childless aunts, I knew nothing of the hard paths that lay ahead. Maybe it was just as well, otherwise I might have packed it all in.

Religion was sacrosanct in the twenties and thirties. The family had become *Annibynwyr* some time during the great religious revival that swept through Wales in the nineteenth century. The word '*Annibynwyr*' can be translated as 'Independent' and compares with the Congregational Church in England. There is no doubt that the revival was a necessity, at a time when debauchery was commonplace, and alcohol, in all its guises, was plentiful and cheap – hence the phrase 'drunk for a penny, dead drunk for tuppence'. I recall seeing an old photograph of about a hundred men and boys gathered on a hillside one Sunday, for the express purpose of imbibing vast quantities of strong ale, and for no other reason than to drink themselves into oblivion. Something had to happen and it did.

The Welsh, as a nation, have never been very ceremoniously inclined and were not enamoured of the pomp, pageantry and incense-swinging ways of the Church of England. So we were ripe for conversion to the practice of a simple religion that was founded on grand oratory. Dead on cue, along came some of the great Welsh preachers of the time. Their platform was the pulpit, from where they denounced the sins of the flesh in ringing tones. Such was their command of words and their presentation that they held their packed chapels spellbound. Many were tall, handsome men with deep stentorian voices, who were admired by men and worshipped by women just as intensely as today's pop stars. I caught the end of the oratorial extravaganza and I can still remember attending a Methodist chapel to hear Tom Nefyn preach. From start to finish his address was hypnotic and, although he spoke for nearly an hour, he commanded our rapt attention. So it was that my generation was born into a constrained world, where pleasure was branded sinful. Simple pastimes such as dancing were frowned upon and I was taught that the only route to heaven was along 'the straight and narrow'. In Sunday School a large picture hung on the wall, depicting the paths to heaven and hell respectively. The righteous trod a narrow path beset with temptations, which they resisted in order to gain entry at the Pearly Gates. The sinners caroused along a broad thoroughfare strewn with pubs, gin palaces, dance halls, gambling joints and other sinful establishments. Everyone seemed to be having a hell of a good time and I wondered, even then, which was destined to be my path and what would be my destination. In retrospect, I think I cut my own track, somewhere in between the broad and the narrow paths and, eventually, I will arrive at – who knows?

In those days, Sunday was a day of rest, and rest one did, come what may. Sunday papers were taboo in our house and even the sewing and knitting were put away in a drawer from Saturday night till Monday morning, but, thankfully, cooking was permitted. Sunday lunch was very nearly a pagan feast. The table sagged under the weight of a huge joint of beef or pork and steaming tureens of boiled and roast potatoes, accompanied by at least two types of vegetables and what seemed to me to be a bath of rich, brown gravy. When we had eaten until we could eat no more, we managed somehow to down a trifle, a fruit tart or whatever, all dripping with thick, sweet custard. The adults then did the washing up, packed me off to Sunday School and collapsed into enormous arm-chairs in the drawing room, where they passed out until I returned an hour later, demanding my tea and home-made cake. I think we gorged ourselves in a kind of defiance to abstinence.

Sunday School played an important role in my young life, as it did in the formative years of all chapel-going children of those times. We were segregated into classes according to age and, before any attempt was made to indoctrinate us into the Christian way of life, we were taught to read. By the time we went to school, at the age of five and not before, we could read and write. As Mother spent most of Sunday morning preparing the gargantuan lunch, we, as a family, attended the six o'clock evening service which, frankly, bored me stiff except for the singing. The whole congregation rose and sang the rousing Welsh hymns with a fervour matched only by the singing at Cardiff Arms Park as sixty thousand voices wait for the home team to emerge to play England. The resident minister took the service, but delegated the prayer to the deacons, in rotation. One of them, a farmer by trade, was exceptional. He knelt, closed his eyes and his voice rose and fell with a musical passion as he begged the Good Lord to forgive us our sins. By the time he had finished, we all knew that we had been cleansed from all evil and that we could sin again on a clean slate!

In fact, religion dominated our lives. It instilled a rigid discipline based on fear, but it was no bad thing for all that. In short, we knew the rules and the consequences if we transgressed. The same disciplinary rules were also applied in the home and in school, with the result that, although there were bouts of childhood mischief, there was no vandalism. We were taught to respect both people and property and found our fun and spent our energies on harmless games and pastimes in a peaceful, well-ordered society.

The highlight of the week for us kids was our Saturday afternoon session at the 'pictures'. The local cinema, known properly as The Pavilion and improperly as Pav, or The Bug House, screened special programmes for us, and for the princely sum of one old penny we were transported from the real world into one of sheer fancy for about an hour and a half. We massed outside the cinema a good half hour before the box-office opened and, in due course, paid our dues and entered the Izal-perfumed auditorium. The Izal was sprayed over the juvenile audience at least twice during the performance to, theoretically, annihilate any fleas and nits that might have entered on our persons. Here it must be admitted that a few of our fellows were a bit flea-ridden. It was a fact of life, and once a week my own head was subjected to the steel-comb torture – a task that Grandma seemed to enjoy. A brass tray with a black underside was inverted on the table, my head was bowed over it and the viciously sharp teeth of the comb were dug into my scalp until they very nearly drew blood. Any foreign bodies that fell on to the tray were promptly despatched with a thumbnail, and I was finally declared bugless, albeit with a scalp that felt as though it had been sand-blasted.

To return to the cinema, our pennyworth allowed us to occupy a series of long, wooden benches in front of the screen. The afternoon's entertainment comprised two films – what we called a 'comic', followed by the hard stuff – a western, or a bloodthirsty cops and robbers. We roared our heads off at the antics of Charlie Chaplin, Laurel and Hardy, Harold Lloyd, Buster Keaton and the Keystone Cops, and screamed encouragement as Tom Mix the cowboy tracked down and vanquished a succession of baddies. We were kept under some measure of control by two elderly attendants, each armed with a cane. I can still hear the swish of that cane as it rent the air, and the thud as it landed on an empty bit of bench; the threat of contact was enough to quell our vocal exuberance, at least temporarily.

They were, of course, silent films with subtitles and accompanied by a piano that played music appropriate to the scene on screen. Tom Mix on his trusty steed sped after the bandits to the tune of 'The Trumpet Voluntary', while something akin to Handel's 'Largo' floated on the air above a love scene, or a death bed. It was great. We were deeply affected by what we saw on the silver screen. An adult, waiting outside the cinema as it disgorged its young audience, had no difficulty in concluding what film had been shown. Following a main-feature cowboy film, we would emerge into the daylight smelling strongly of Izal and walking like John Wayne, and after seeing Al Jolson in *Danny Boy*, we hit the street in total silence, ashamed of our puffed, red-rimmed eyes. Then the 'talkies' came to Cardigan. It was sensational. Those who couldn't read the subtitles could now follow he plot, and it transformed their lives! People came from far and wide to see the first showing of the talking film and the cinema put on two houses nightly to cope with the crowds. It was such an historic event that my grandmother, who didn't hold with 'pictures', threw her principles to the wind and joined Mother and I on the First Night. Strangely enough, I have little recollection of that film, with the exception of a vague memory of biplanes shooting at each other and that the principal hero was George Arliss – I think. I've no idea what Grandmother thought of it, but she never set foot in a cinema again, although I was still allowed my Saturday afternoon debauchery, even when the admission price shot up 50 per cent to a 'pennyhappeny'. To be fair, I was always given a halfpenny over the ticket price, so that I could treat myself to the tempting tubes of sherbet with liquorice straws that were purveyed at half-time by a young lady wielding a laden tray beneath an ample bosom.

They were happy, carefree days for me and for most of my friends, but not for all. There was very real poverty in the town and the poor were hard put to exist, let alone enjoy life. I attended the Board School in a class of twenty or so pupils, some of whom were dressed in hand-me-downs and had never known the luxury of a square meal. They relied heavily on the generosity of kindly people and on official hand-outs. Social Security was still in the distant future and I remember some of my fellow pupils being given tickets in school entitling them to attend the soup kitchen, where they were presented with a bowl of hot nutritious soup and a thick slice of bread. Keeping warm in winter in old draughty houses was another problem the poor faced with amazing fortitude. The price of coal was far beyond their means, but yet another ticket from the authorities allowed them to call at the gasworks and collect a bag of coke each week. The yawning abyss between the rich, the 'no-worries' and the poor was not evident to us youngsters. We all attended the same school, we played and fought together, and it seemed only natural to share a few sweets with a less fortunate friend.

The Board School is now a car-park and I, for one, bemoan its passing. It was conveniently situated, just two minutes from home, and Johnny Davies' sweet shop was even more conveniently situated across the road. There were three classes – the Infants, the Middle Class and the Seniors, who were coached to sit and, hopefully, pass the entrance examination to the Grammar School. I began my education in the Infants under the gaze of a kindly old (she seemed old to me) lady called Miss Williams. Our class was adjacent to the Senior class and separated from it by a half-timber, half-glass-paned partition. The seniors came under the thumb and jurisdiction of the headmaster, John Evans, a good teacher, but subject to fits of violent temper. We cowered in terror when his voice rose to a deafening crescendo, and on at least one occasion the formidable wooden pointer he used shattered a pane of glass in the partition and very nearly ended the scholastic future of a member of our class. It was just as well that his aim did not match his temper, otherwise half his class would not have survived to sit their exams. He was also a man of mystery. On many Friday evenings after school he would go home, change his garb and, equipped with a stout walking stick, set out on foot from Cardigan to Aberystwyth, a distance of thirty-eight miles; he made the return trip on Sunday. What he did and how he spent his time in 'Aber' are matters of speculation!

All this time my health was still a matter of concern to the family. Although the TB had been cured, I was a comparative weakling. I caught colds with consummate ease and every germ in the area found in me an unwilling but receptive host. I was laid low with 'flu, laryngitis, scarlet fever, measles (both German and British), chicken-pox and anything else that happened to be in the air, including tonsilitis. So it was decided that I would be better off without my tonsils, which were thought to be vestigial and useless. I was told by the doctor and all the family that the operation would be painless and that I would not suffer in any way. They were downright liars, all of them.

There was, and there still is, a hospital in Cardigan but, for some reason that I cannot fathom, the operation to remove the offending organs was carried out on the kitchen table. The family doctor wielded the knife and the qualified nurse in attendance was one of the aunts. The table was scrubbed down and a rubber sheet placed over it. I was stretched out on the sheet and a further sheet of rubber covered my frailty from neck to toe. Then, what appeared to be a large tea-strainer was lined with cotton-wool and semi-saturated with chloroform. It was placed over my breathing apparatus and I was instructed to inhale deeply and to exhale slowly. I did, the world swam briefly and, as expected, I passed out. When I came to, I was minus my tonsils and plus one hell of a sore throat. It was several days before I was able to utter a word.

My only means of communication was via a sheet of paper on which my grandma had printed the alphabet, and I indicated my needs by spelling them out with my finger. My throat was too tender to allow for the passage of solids and the doctor had decreed that I was to be fed only with liquids and (God bless him) ice-cream. On hearing this, my aunts assumed the role of ice-cream bearers. They probably got together and worked out a rota system, because never a day passed without a convoy of loving aunts appearing in my bedroom, armed with basins of vanilla, strawberry and raspberry flavours, bought at Conti's ice-cream parlour in the High Street. I began to believe that tonsillectomy was not so bad after all. In accordance with accepted practice, my adenoids had also been removed and, as things were in those days, they would probably have knifed my appendix as well, had it been nearer my throat.

The operation was obviously a success, as shortly afterwards I began to ward off disease, put on weight and height and assume the appearance of a healthy little boy. Alas, my troubles were not yet over. After a year or so I went into recession and, once again, became prone to pestilence. I couldn't believe my ears when our doctor took me on his knee and, in a voice heavy with syrup, told me that I would have to have my tonsils out a second time. I and the family were deeply distressed and mystified by the news. The obvious questions were asked. Where had these other tonsils come from? What had he (the doctor) removed last time, if the self-same organs were still present? Had he been drunk, inefficient, or both at the same time of the first operation? In fairness, Dr Davies was the epitome of sobriety and also a nice, fatherly figure with a faultless bedside manner. Obviously, I don't remember his explanation, but I gather it went something like this: at that time tonsils were hard-pruned and not removed by the roots, as they are nowadays. Consequently, the stumps had shown new growth and developed side-shoots and further pruning was necessary. With fond memories of copious quantities of ice-cream, I agreed to a second ordeal, which was performed at the hospital. Once again, the aunts rallied round, but with less enthusiasm than previously and there were days when I went for over an hour before the ice-cold elixir of life was placed before me! Although not yet seven years old, I had suffered much, triumphed over my early adversities and have been amply rewarded with health of body and mind ever since. As a result of my juvenile misfortunes, I do not take health for granted. Daily, I thank the Good Lord for it and, as far as I am concerned, health is synonymous with happiness.

In the 1920s life was slow, smooth and fairly static in West Wales. To travel any distance we used the Great Western Railway steam trains, and for local transport we relied almost entirely on the bicycle, the horse and cart, or pony and trap. A trap was a two-wheeled vehicle, equipped with a bench seat on each side and a pair of formidable brass paraffin lamps. They, and the high-stepping ponies that pulled them, were a source of great pride to their owners, and both were kept in immaculate condition. The woodwork was waxed and polished, the metalwork shone like a beacon, and the pony was brushed until its coat gleamed and it was often dressed with ribbons. It was a smart turnout and the pony knew it. It held its head high and the more people there were around, the more it pranced and gestured. Not to be outdone, the cart-horses had their day on Barley Saturday. On this farmers' fair-day the horses were gorgeously groomed. With not a hair out of place, their long manes were plaited and ribboned, and the brasses and harnesses shone with blinding brilliance. They were paraded through the streets and I swear they enjoyed their annual, brief incursion into the unaccustomed limelight.

I was still under school age when I made my first journey in a bus. It must have been a momentous occasion, otherwise the mental picture I still have would not have been so indelibly etched on my memory. It was, I believe, the town's first venture into the realms of public transport and it was owned and operated by the GWR company. It ran from the northern limits of Cardigan down the main street to the station on the southern limits, a distance of about one and a half miles. Sporting the railway company's sombre brown and yellow colours, it had solid rubber tyres, and the seating accommodation comprised two long wooden benches, one on each side of the interior. In other words, it was a boneshaker. But for a small boy, it was a thrilling journey into the unknown. Mother and I boarded the vehicle at the Victoria Gardens stop, travelled to the station, got out, got back in again and rattled back to our point of embarkation. What a thrill that was!

Motor cars were few and very far between, so few, in fact, that we children viewed them with awe. There were no parking problems in those days. Drivers left their vehicles wherever it was convenient and didn't bother to remove the keys from the ignition, because there weren't any, and, anyway, no one was likely to purloin the vehicle. By the time a thief had got the thing going, the police would have arrived with time to spare. The first car in our family was a bull-nosed Morris Cowley that Uncle John, the auctioneer, bought to facilitate his business activities. Besides shouting the odds at the local cattle mart, he had to visit farms that came up for sale, to value their stock and chattels. From time to time, I was accorded the privilege of accompanying him on his travels, which made me the envy of all my schoolmates. On one unforgettable day he took us all to Tenby, a daring distance of thirty-two miles. 'Us' included Grandmother, Mother, me and Father, who happened to be home on shore-leave. Male superiority (so-called) decreed that Father sat in the front with the driver, while the ladies and I were sardined into the open dickey at the rear. The journey to Tenby was great. It was new and exciting, the day was fine and sunny and I knew that the picnic hamper held my favourite foods and enough pop to keep me going. We picnicked on Tenby's golden sands, we played games, built the compulsory sand-castles and paddled in the clear, unpolluted sea. Departure for home was scheduled for six o'clock. We packed our paraphernalia, cleared our litter, climbed the steep steps up to the promenade and arranged ourselves in the Morris, ready for the off. Unfortunately, 'Morris' had other ideas. It liked Tenby and flatly refused to start. Father and Uncle John took it in turns – one to crank the starting handle, whilst the other one fiddled with the throttle lever on the steering column. 'Morris' remained obstinate and refused to produce a spark of life. Eventually, a small army of sympathetic volunteers heaved and pushed old 'Morris' until he gave up the struggle and spluttered into life. A mighty cheer went up, we all climbed on board and set off for home.

By this time the setting sun was dipping into the watery horizon and there was a decided nip in the air. In the dickey, the three of us felt the full blast of the cold night air, and by the time we reached our destination we were very close to hypothermia. Uncle John and Father had to prise us out of our cold, cramped quarters, and the ladies swore they would never venture on such precarious journeys ever again. Hot cups of tea and plates of eggs and bacon soon restored our flagging spirits, and by the following morning all I could remember was the fun, the frenetic return journey having paled into insignificance. Strange how the human mind seems capable of recalling only the sunny side of life and of locking the darker side away in recesses that need never be opened, except by special request. I confess to many such depositories of morbid memory, and in the writing of this book it will be necessary to open some of the locked doors on reluctant recall. Fortunately, the hinges are well-oiled and the doors will be slammed shut much quicker than they are opened.

Up to the age of seven I had been the object of devoted, undivided love, but in January 1931 something happened that threw a large spanner into my self-centred works. The day began like any other. I rose from my bed, washed, dressed and went downstairs for breakfast, to be told that mother was not well and was staying in bed. I pleaded to see her, but was told that a nurse was in attendance and my presence was forbidden. One of the aunts cooked my breakfast and I left for school a very worried young man. I had never known my mother to suffer a day's illness and her present indisposition seemed inexplicable, as she had appeared to be hale and hearty the previous day.

CLAY

All was revealed when I returned from school. The house was full of aunts – they were everywhere – and I was told that I was such a lucky little boy – I had a sister! To be honest, I didn't feel the least bit lucky and I failed to understand why the arrival of my sister, Margaret, had coincided with my mother's illness. It was a golden opportunity for someone to put me in the picture, to set out the fundamental facts of life, but nobody did. In a noncomformist household in those days, sex, along with swearing and strong drink, was taboo, so I was left in ignorance. In fact, I already had a satisfactory, but erroneous view of where babies came from. Grandmother was an inveterate hoarder and, among other things, she kept every picture-postcard that came through the letterbox. One of them (I can see it now) was a view of a cabbage patch and the head of a beaming baby smiled from the heart of every plant. Small wonder that I believed that I had been born of a Brassica. I stumbled on the far more exiting truth a few years later. In the meantime, I considered my new-found sister a horticultural product and deeply resented her intrusion into my previously well-ordered and exclusive life. In short, I thought she was a damned nuisance.

Little boys of seven are noisy, and so was I. On my return from school or play, I didn't just open the door and walk in. I threw it open, burst through and, in stentorian tones, demanded to be fed, or imparted news of the latest wildly exciting event of the day. The response to my youthful exuberance was invariably, 'Shh, the baby's asleep.' I could have cheerfully strangled her! Furthermore, Margaret replaced me in my mother's affections and only my grandmother's continued devotion saved me from becoming a lifelong misogynist. It was not my sister's fault, of course. It was just that a seven-year age-gap made for total incompatibility and, although the gap has narrowed to an imperceptible fissure with the passing years, it is still there. The bond of genetic inheritance is strong, however. Margaret and I will spring to each other's aid or defence without hesitation, but we have never been what is, in common parlance, close. A great pity, but there it is. The strange thing is that, had our roles been reversed, things could have been very different. I know families where the girl is older than the boy by several years and a strong bond exists between them, probably because most girls are born with mothering instincts and a baby boy is as welcome and acceptable as a new doll.

Grandmother's influence on my early life and subsequently was profound. We loved each other dearly. She exercised a subtle, gentle but firm discipline that has stood me in good stead all my life. Widowed in her early thirties, she donned widow's weeds for all her remaining years. As far as she was concerned, there was only one man in her life and, although he had passed on, she kept his loving memory alive in her heart for all time. In her way of life and dress she was immaculate. She was small of stature, fine-boned and dainty, yet her daily appearance in the breakfast room was little short of majestic. She dressed all in black, relieved only by the subdued, coloured pattern of her bodice, and her feather-fine hair was swept up into a top knot, held in place with a pretty comb. She followed a strict routine that never varied, which made for an orderly, untroubled life. She was also a very determined lady. In her forties she had been stricken with a severe attack of gastric flu. During and immediately following her recovery her doctor had prescribed a strict diet, until she was restored to health. Grandmother, being Grandmother, reckoned that, as the diet had worked the oracle, she should stick to it all her days and she did, never once being tempted by the consumable luxuries that the rest of us enjoyed. She let Mother do the cooking, probably because she had no idea how to do it. On the farm the maids had prepared the meals and seen to most of the household chores, leaving the matriarch to oversee the staff and their duties. No longer having staff to supervise and instruct, she commanded my mother instead. Mother prepared our meals, saw to the beds and the upstairs, while Grandmother did the dusting, the silver and brass and a general tidy-up downstairs. Lunch was at twelve noon on the dot, and in the afternoon Grandma sat by the fire, knitting, sewing or reading her *Christian Herald*. She sewed buttons back on my shirts, repaired the cavernous holes in my socks, knitted new ones and even polished my boots, ready for the following day. Mother either knitted, or spent an hour or two in the garden on fine days. Tea and home-made buns were served at four o'clock, to be followed at six by high-tea-cum-dinner, called supper. This last meal of the day was pot-luck, depending on what was readily available. In summer, salads were frequent and delicious, and in winter there were various fry-ups, or *cawl*.

Cawl is exclusively Welsh and remotely akin to a broth, or thick soup. The initial, essential ingredients are a very large saucepan, water and – the *pièce de résistance* – a large piece of beef, preferably on the bone. This is simmered slowly until tender, then the meat is removed and the vegetables added. Potatoes, carrots and swedes are followed by shredded cabbage or Brussels sprouts and, last of all, the leeks. Thyme and parsley are added to this mixture and the whole lot is brought back to the boil and then simmered on, or near, the open fire for ever! Well, not quite for ever, but certainly all winter long and, as the level falls, so the stock pot is replenished, maintaining a constant supply of nutritious, delicious, belly-warming food. The *cawl* is served accompanied by thick slices of the cold beef and chunks of home-made bread. A memorable meal, guaranteed to repel winter's gloom and disorders.

Except on Sundays, the frying pan was in constant use, with everything cooked in beef or pork fat and, since I still live and breathe, it couldn't have played havoc with my metabolism. After the day's final repast, I did my homework and the ladies sat by the fireside, chatting, reading – nothing strenuous, just relaxing. At 8.30 p.m. precisely, Grandmother got out her Bible and read a chapter. At 8.45 p.m., Mother put the kettle on and, when it was near the boil, she filled a large cup, lit a candle and took both to Grandmother, who was reaching the last verse of her biblical reading. At the stroke of nine, she rose from her armchair, took cup and candle, bade us goodnight and, as regally as she had begun her day, she daintily trod the stairs to bed. Her regime never varied and, as she lived to a ripe old age, there's much to be said for her ordered, peaceful and untrammelled way of life.

Callers were frequent and warmly welcomed. They never used the knocker, because they knew that the door was unlocked. So they just opened it and yelled the Welsh equivalent of 'Hello there', to be greeted by an equally loud invitation to come on in. Mother was always glad of a chat and a chance to catch up on the latest, juicy gossip, and so too was Grandmother, providing the callers were Welsh. On the rare occasions when an English person dropped in, she rapidly disappeared into the kitchen and stayed there until the visitor had departed. Her precipitate vanishing act was not prompted by racism or anything, she simply didn't understand or converse very well in English. For that matter, neither did I, until I went to primary school and began to learn a language that was as foreign to me as Arabic. I soon learnt that *'cath'* was 'cat' and *'ci'* was 'dog', but I and my contemporaries had the greatest difficulty in mastering the pronunciation of longer English words. I could never understand why a word spelt 'cough' was pronounced 'coff', while 'bough' became 'bow' and not 'boff', as I was entitled to expect. Furthermore, the plural of 'mouse' is 'mice', therefore, more than one 'grouse' should be 'grice', but no – it is still 'grouse', whether it is only one or a moorful of the darned birds. Being a phonetic language, the pronunciation of all Welsh words is easy and straightforward, once you've learnt the alphabet. Nevertheless, I am bound to admit that the language of my fathers is beset with grammatical hurdles, not the least of which is that, as in French, things are either male or female, not just 'it' as in English. For example, a chair is *'cadair'* and, in referring to it, I would say, *'y gadair hon'* – the hard C transmuting to a soft G and the *hon* indicating its feminine gender. I still get it wrong at times, but once I'd learnt the essential difference between the human male and female, in any language, I can't say I was bothered!

Before closing the chapter on my first nine years, I recount an incident that caused much embarrassment at the time. Mother and I were walking down Cardigan High Street and, as we drew level with a motorbike, it backfired with a crack of thunder only a yard or so from my right ear. I shot several feet into the air and from that moment, acquired an acute stammer. I became the butt of my classmates' inhuman cruelty and the family practically disowned me. Normal conversation became almost impossible when I was present and, when anyone called, I was despatched to my bedroom and ordered to stay there until the coast was clear. My stuttered existence continued for several weeks until my grandmother, in her worldly wisdom, found the remedy. She took me to one side and told me that she and I would conduct a musical conversation until I could string my words together normally. So we both sang our sentences, she in a soft soprano and I likewise, and without a trace of a stammer. In a matter of days my speech impediment had completely disappeared and I was reinstated into the normal world.

It is held that a person's character, behaviour and outlook are moulded during the first few formative years, and I firmly believe this to be true. In the home and within the confines of the community I found love, I felt secure and I was taught the basic rudiments of self-discipline. I missed the paternal presence of my father, much more than I knew, but the warmth of the family's love more than compensated for his long absences. I was taught the difference between right and wrong, both in the home and in the chapel, quite painlessly. Of course I transgressed from time to time (what child doesn't?) and when I did misbehave, I was verbally chastised and made to promise that I would not repeat the misdemeanour. As Grandmother said, 'A broken promise breaks a heart.' I believed her; I still do, and to this day the few pledges I have broken, mostly inadvertently, have been causes of lasting concern. A sense of security is vital in a child's life. I knew, without being told, that succour and safety dwelt behind the front door of home. The house was never empty when I returned from school or play. Food and warmth were there for the taking, and any problems I had dissolved into thin air when I shared them with Mother and Grandmother. I was a lucky little boy and, although I didn't know it then, I certainly know it now.

A New Life

$\mathscr{P}$

'THE moving finger writes and, having writ, moves on', and so did I. The next nine years were full to overflowing with new experiences, contradictions, deep emotional disturbances and days of unimaginable happiness. In the town, life had been constrained by concrete. I was a street-wise kid who ventured forth into the countryside and towards the coast all too infrequently. In 1932, fate decreed that my horizons were to be extended dramatically, and to my positive advantage.

The late twenties and early thirties were hard times. A slump hit right into the very heart of Britain. Strikes, unemployment and depression were the order of the day, and our family did not escape the general deprivation. Father's ship, with countless others, was laid up. In other words, it unloaded its cargo, leaving the holds empty and, international trade being at a low ebb, they remained empty. The ship was then taken from the quayside, anchored in the harbour approaches and abandoned until trading recovered and it could be brought back into service. The whole crew, including Father, was paid off and that was that. I was too young to appreciate the seriousness of the situation, although even I sensed the gloom that pervaded our household. Father was still his kindly, considerate self, but he wore a worried frown, as did the two women in my life. Our meals became more frugal, bus trips to the seaside were non-existent. Uncle John's auctioneering business went bust and Grandmother was busier than ever, darning and repairing worn and overworn clothing.

Something had to be done and Mother, being a very practical lady, did it. The town house was sold for £750 and we moved to a small farm, seven miles north of Cardigan. Mother reasoned that the farm could feed us at the very least, and hoped that the surplus of produce would provide a source of income. The sale of the house provided enough ready cash to stock the smallholding with four cows, a pig and an initial consignment of day-old chicks, with, I believe, a hundred pounds or two left over to meet day-to-day expenses. We were in business. The odd thing was that the town house had been bought by the Timothys who lived directly opposite in the same street. I am still puzzled as to why they should wish to move such a short distance, from one side of the street to the other. Maybe it was because the house they had lived in for many, many years backed on to the cinema and, with the advent of the 'talking pictures', they had got fed up with the noise of the constant warfare between cowboys and Indians, and the gunfire as Al Capone and his ilk fought off the forces of law and order. It could have been that!

It was about this time that I became aware that, in our family, money was spelt MONEY. I gathered from adult conversation that Grandmother had been 'done out' of her rightful share of some inheritance or other by a near relative and it rankled. To make matters worse, she had invested most of the proceeds from the sale of her farm in her youngest son's business and when that failed, the family cupboard was left almost as bare as Uncle Griff's bald head. So it was that the acquisition of cash and the restoration of a healthy bank balance overrode all other facts and ways of life. Money became an end in itself, rather than a means to an end and, even in my greenest of salad days, I felt that this should not be so. The underlying cause of the family's pursuit of pence, shillings and pounds sprang from the alien feeling of insecurity that came from being, not exactly in the red, but of being only faintly in the black for the first time in their lives. The family fortunes were soon modestly restored, but a sense of insecurity remained. Furthermore, it was drummed into me that 'never a lender nor a borrower be'. I was told and taught that anything I couldn't pay for, I should do without. It made sound sense then and it still does.

I have digressed merely to underline the family's commitment to financial security and independence, which prompted our move from town to country. I was kept in the dark about our exodus until the day before it happened, when I couldn't help noticing that our goods and chattels were being packed into numerous tea chests. On the following morning a large open lorry arrived, was loaded and departed, carrying Father, Mother, my sister and about a third of our worldly goods. Grandmother and I were left to guard the remainder and to supervise the loading of lots two and three. The move was made in October and, by the time the last load was secured, it was dark and cold. Grandma sat in the front, wedged between the driver and his mate, and I was squeezed into a gap between a chest of drawers and something else by the tailboard. I had been given a very important commission. I was appointed to hold in my safe-keeping a paraffin lamp, whose significance I was to realise when we reached our destination. That seven-mile journey was sheer agony. I couldn't move. I couldn't even rub my hands together to keep my circulation going. When we arrived at the farm, I was totally immobile, paralysed with cold, but the lamp was intact. I was plied with tea and food, my limbs were massaged, the blood flowed and I took stock of my situation. Frankly, I didn't like what I saw.

To begin with, there was no electricity. All right, we didn't have electricity in Cardigan either, but at least we did have gas on the ground floor, where the lamps gave forth light when a chain was pulled and a match applied to the mantel – but not here. The only means of illumination were the paraffin lamp and candles. The worst was to come – there was no running water and, by inference, no taps, no bathroom and no flush toilet. The only source of water was a pipe that protruded from a stone wall about fifty yards from the back door, and the water had to be lugged to the kitchen in two 2-gallon cans.

As we were now seven miles from the nearest gasometer, the cooking was done either on the open fire, in the oven alongside, or on a paraffin stove. The one and only lavatory was a corrugated-iron 'sentry box', positioned at the far end of the garden under an Allington Pippin apple tree. It consisted of a single-seater wooden board over a bucket; although on some farms I visited later, the WCs were two-seater – how friendly can you get?! I remember a standing joke of the time that may well have had an element of truth in it: an English town family wrote in reply to an advertisement offering a Welsh farmhouse holiday and enquired whether there was a WC. In Welsh a lavatory is a *ty bach* and, being Methodists and Welsh-speaking, the farmer's wife wrote back with the information that there was a WC in the village with a seating capacity of over two hundred. She had interpreted WC as Wesleyan Chapel, and nothing further was heard from the 'townies'.

Our WC looked a picture in spring, wreathed in apple blossom, but on windy autumn nights the clunk of apples falling on the tin roof sounded like an artillery barrage. Little did I know on that first night, that it would fall to my lot to dig holes in the nearest field, into which to empty the contents of the bucket. Looking back, I'm surprised that we didn't suffer severe constipation during the winter months when we were reluctant to leave the warmth of the hearth, to make the muddy, slithery trip to the 'thunderbox' in cold, pouring rain, with only a torch to guide us. Grandmother, of course, 'made her own arrangements'!

For me, bath night was Friday night. As I had done ever since I was old enough, I waited until everyone was in bed, then I half-filled a large zinc tub with cold water and added saucepanfuls of hot water until it reached the necessary comfortable temperature. The hot water came from a small cistern that was an integral part of the kitchen range, along with a large oven. The fire never went out. It was stoked with culm and was kept going in summer and winter for the convenience of instant hot water and for simple cooking and tea-making. Culm was a cheap, slow-burning fuel that consisted of an odd mixture of coal-dust and a type of clay, called marl. It was delivered ready-mixed by lorry and unceremoniously dumped in the yard adjacent to one of the outhouses. It was humped inside by wheelbarrow and prepared for use a bucketful at a time, by adding water until it had the consistency of thick mud. The amorphous mess was carried to the kitchen and, during the day, moulded by hand into balls that were arranged on the already burning fire. The stoking system changed last thing before going to bed. Instead of culm balls, the whole surface of the fire was cased with a two-inch-deep layer of the stuff and a small hole was pokered in the centre, to allow gases to escape up the chimney. In the morning the fire looked as dead as a December dormouse, but all that one had to do was rake out the fine ash at the bottom, break up the surface crust and the fire obligingly burst into life. This was the primitive existence that, at the tender age of nine, I had thrust upon me.

Soon the modern conveniences of our town house were but a memory and, come to think of it, the 'convenience' was no longer convenient. In the darkness of my first night in Ty-Cornel I was distressed and depressed beyond measure. Owls hooted and the wind whispered threats through the bare branches of the oak outside my bedroom window. I couldn't sleep a wink. I felt forlorn and lost in foreign territory and the thought of escape crossed my mind. But, if I ran away, where could I go? Who would have me? Who would feed my ravenous frame, and on this thought a vision of bacon and eggs came into view. I decided to wait until after breakfast before doing anything precipitous and, in that frame of mind, I fell into a fitful sleep.

Fortunately, day one dawned bright and sunny and I took stock of my surroundings. In the light of day the kitchen was warm and welcoming, and after a hearty breakfast I went on a tour of the 'estate'. I discovered that we had four large fields and two smaller ones, one with a well in it. There was also a stream and a pond with a resident family of moorhens. The hedgerows were pock-marked with rabbit warrens and, to my delight, I surprised several of the furry beasties cavorting in the morning sunshine. There were several outhouses to explore, and by lunchtime I was converted to country life. From a tremulous townie, I became a learner country yokel in the space of a few hours. I now know that life began for me from that moment. Nature and I met each other for the first time that morning. She bade me welcome and I, for my part, began to learn her ways and respect her laws.

Mother, in her wisdom, decreed that I could be excused school for a week, the better to acclimatise myself to everything that was so new. She also guessed that the arrival of the animals would thrill me to bits, and she was right. On the Monday following the Friday of the move, a cattle truck arrived and disgorged two cows – a Friesian and a Hereford. Mother, not being the most imaginative of women, promptly christened the Friesian, 'Friesian', but let her imagination run riot with the other and bestowed on her the title 'Daisy'. Daisy was a typical Herefordshire beast – quiet and independent; Friesian was entirely different. She was intelligent, frolicsome and in search of a friend, and in me she found her soul mate. We became great pals. Whenever I entered her field, she would gallop towards me, kicking her hind legs high in the air and coming to a halt little more than a yard or so from me. It was her way of expressing her joy at our meeting. If she happened to be lying prone on the grass, she would allow me to sit astride her back, then rise and take me for a sedate walk around the field, or down to the cowshed, if it was milking time. Her complete trust in me became evident when I noticed that all was not well with her. She became morose, hung her head and in her stall she pressed it hard against the woodwork. Looking at her, it dawned on me that her right horn had grown backwards against her skull. Closer examination showed that it was pressing with considerable pressure against the bone immediately above her eye. The pain must have been excruciating and the situation called for swift action. I fetched a hacksaw, spoke to her softly, explained what I was about to do, took a firm hold on the offending horn and began to saw.

33

She didn't make a move during the whole operation, and when it was over, her rough, red tongue came out and I received a very wet lick on my cheek. Friesian was the first animal to demonstrate for me the warmth and affection that can and should exist between man and beast. There have been many more since, but my first love affair with an animal was with gentle, good-natured Friesian.

Two more cows came within a week, and the four-stall cowshed was full to capacity. The first was a docile Jersey we called – yes, you've guessed it – 'Jersey', and the second was a blue-grey Irish beast named 'Paddy'. She was a bitch – there's no other word to describe her. She distrusted and bore a grudge against all humanity, and against me in particular. She was always reluctant to enter the cowshed and had to be coaxed into her stall, preferring to squat in any of the others. When I eventually got her installed, she would allow me to place the rope halter around her neck, then, when I tried to retreat between her and her neighbour, Jersey, she would deliberately move sideways, so that I was sandwiched between them. As I fought for breath and to free myself, she would turn her head, and the look in her eyes was one of evil, sadistic pleasure. We milked Friesian, Daisy and Jersey with consummate ease. They happily munched the sweet-smelling hay, while Mother kneaded their teats and teased the warm, fresh milk into the bucket. Paddy was made of sterner stuff. She had two weapons at her disposal – her tail and her back legs. She would show her displeasure by swishing her tail across the face of the milker and, since cows cannot kick sideways, she would wait until the bucket was half-full, then lift her leg and plonk her dirty hoof right into it. We got the better of her by tying her tail to one of her legs and then strapping both hind legs together. Needless to say, I was the one who did the tying and strapping, while mother began milking the placid bovines. It became a twice-daily battle of wits. Paddy was well aware of my intentions and lay in wait. Somehow I always managed to get the strap round her legs from the side and once that was accomplished, it wasn't difficult to trap her flailing tail and anchor it to her hind quarters. Only once did she catch me unawares. I had unhitched her immobility with unusual ease, prior to turning her out of the cowshed, and I made the fatal mistake of losing my concentration. The task done, I passed behind her and, timing her stroke to perfection, she lashed out and her hoof caught me on my kneecap with the force of a Scud missile. I was thrown back against the cowshed door and I swear that she-devil cow actually smirked. We sold her soon after that.

The remainder of our livestock were dull in comparison. A young pig arrived and was housed in a newly whitewashed pigsty. Mother bought a box or two of day-old chicks and they took up residence in a paraffin-powered, heated incubator in one of the outhouses. Then we experienced our first taste of the friendly, close-knit community that we had entered. On only our second evening in the farmhouse, a knock came on the door and there stood a neighbouring farmer with a hen in each hand. With an embarrassed half-smile, he proclaimed the birds a gift 'to get you started', as he put it. Four more hens and a cockerel arrived in similar and rapid succession. Father fashioned very adequate nest-boxes out of some orange crates that were knocking about, and within a day or two we had our first Brown Leghorn egg. Our production line was in motion and it verified our belief that the future was bound to be rosy, as indeed it proved to be. How could it have been otherwise among simple, kindly folk who breathed the clean air, led the good life and lived off the land? I slipped effortlessly into the communal, compassionate stream and drifted along between its timeless banks as to the manner born.

Ironically, within a year or so of leaving town, international trade picked up, Father's ship was recommissioned and we waved farewell to him once more. At the age of eleven I became the male head of the household and, among my other duties, I was appointed IC MANURE. In other words, it fell to my lot to barrow the cow droppings from the cowshed to the *tomen* (manure heap) and, in due season, to barrow the oldest, richest, composted, natural fertiliser to the gardens.

Ty-Cornel boasted two gardens, and the one by the house was the vegetable garden, conveniently sited a few yards from our home-produced fertiliser. We grew lashings of sweet and succulent vegetables and fruit, using nothing more than natural plant food. I learnt – and am still convinced – that the best and most efficient fertiliser factory in the world is the cow. Grass, which is plentiful, goes in one end, rich, organic fertiliser comes out the other end, and in between there's a milk bar. What an animal!

Our other garden was mostly a well-established orchard with space for still more vegetables and a few flowers that were grown for cutting. To my delight I was allocated my very own vegetable plot and thus began my lifelong love of growing things. I bought my first packets of seeds – lettuce and radish – and, with a little guidance from mother, I sowed them, watched them germinate and grow and eventually, and with inestimable pride, brought them to be cooked and consumed. Seeds have fascinated me ever since. They are so small, and look so lifeless and uninteresting, yet put them to soil and warmth and moisture in the spring, and with the sap they emerge from the subterranean darkness to feed our hunger and delight our senses with their beauty and fragrance – such little things, giving so much pleasure. Now, nearly sixty years on, the annual miracle of Nature's rebirth each spring is as exciting and as new to me as it ever was.

My first week on the farm was an age of discovery, the second came close to disaster – I went to school. Being of farming stock, my grandfather and Uncle John had worn breeches and leggings – sensible, practical garb for muddy yards and fields. These leggings were made of the finest leather and encased the leg from ankle to about two or three inches below the knee. To safeguard my nether regions from cold and wet, it was decided that I should be equipped with a pair of made-to-measure black leggings. In addition, my footwear had to be a pair of stout, black hob-nailed boots. On the evening prior to my first day in the new school the leggings and boots were polished to Grenadier Guards standard and, in high spirits, I set off for Glynarthen Elementary School – two miles distant. I walked tall, proud of my spick and span appearance and totally unaware of what was to confront me at the school gates. The village of Glynarthen sleeps its days away in a quiet valley. In the early thirties there was a chapel, a shop-cum-post office, a clog-maker, the school and about ten or twelve houses. A few of the school-children hailed from the village, but the vast majority walked in from the outlying farms. The boys and girls wore sensible country clothing and iron-rimmed, wooden clogs. My too-immaculate black-legginged, black-booted appearance was greeted by incredulous stares, quickly followed by raucous laughter and screams of derision. I realise now that I must have stood out like a ham roll in a synagogue. I had unconsciously broken the mould, infringed the tenets of attire, and I had to be punished. Day after day I suffered taunts and insults. I bore them with a degree of fortitude until finally I cracked and, in a fit of momentary rage, traded insult for insult with the pack-leader, who promptly challenged me to a fight when school was over for the day. Conscious that the good name of the Clays and Joneses had to be upheld, I couldn't refuse. After school we all trooped off up the lane, found a secluded venue and 'Bighead' and I squared up to each other in a ring of twenty or more excited kids, all yelling encouragement to no one in particular. Never having fought anyone in my life before, I was uncertain of my first move. I needn't have worried. Pack-leader (I can't remember his name) threw a punch and caught me behind the ear. Incensed, I threw one back and landed a beauty on his nose. He was so surprised that he stepped back, tripped over a pothole, fell to the ground and there and then lost his throne and crown. Defeated and deflated, he gave in, as bullies do, and I was accepted into the juvenile hierarchy. In that lane, on that day, I learnt that bullies are paper heroes and that justice and fair play are not ours for the asking; they have to be earned, even fought for.

Now one of the gang, school was great and I looked forward to the daily two-mile trek there and back. There were no school buses, no perils on the way and no school meals. My morning

satchel held my homework and a tin box containing sandwiches of either cheese, jam or paste and a medicine bottle full
of milk. Mr Davies the Head was a superb teacher and, beside
doing the three Rs routine, he took us on nature walks, and
we had our own small plots in the school kitchen garden. I
learnt the names of the flowers of the fields and hedgerows
and how to detect the signs of animal life and to identify
myriad insects.

In spring the high banks shone with pale yellow splashes of
colour as primroses heralded longer days and warmer
weather. In summer's heat blue scabious, red campions and
herb-Robert kept us company on our journeys, and the scent
of meadow-sweet was so strong, I could have bottled it. The
fields and hedgerows were a-flutter with butterflies of all
kinds – Red Admirals, Brimstones, Wood Whites, Peacocks,
and on one unforgettable day I saw one of the loveliest creatures I've ever set eyes on. Walking up a shady lane I passed
under an overhanging branch, happened to glance up and
there, on the underside of a leaf, rested a Silver-Washed Frit-
illary, its large, black-pattered, brown wings pulsating almost
imperceptibly in a shaft of sunlight. I was transfixed, hardly
breathing, and the lovely creature folded its wings to reveal
the silvery under-sheen. Moments like that are prized and
precious – brief encounters with a breathtaking beauty that
only Nature paints.

I was fascinated and continued to study the changing flora
and fauna of the hedgerows on my journeys to and from
school. It was on one such voluntary scanning of the hedges
that I detected a slight movement and went closer to inves-
tigate. There, concealed among the grass, the scabious, the
harebells and the toadflax, was a tiny, terrified, ginger kitten.
It was too weak to move, and gave an almost inaudible mew
of protest as I lifted her up and tucked her into my satchel.
Actually it was a him, not a her, but how was I to know?

Mother was also an animal lover and within minutes of my
arrival home Pussy was ravenously supping warm, fresh milk.
It was only then that I noticed that the kitten's ginger coat was

caked and rock-hard. I christened him 'Toots' and tried to work out what could have happened to solidify his fir. There were two possible solutions: he had either fallen into a bucket of pig swill, which normally consisted of water thickened with flour or meal, together with potato peelings, cabbage leaves and other bits and pieces, or he had been thrown in. Farm cats were a promiscuous bunch and begat with monotonous and embarrassing frequency. Regrettably, the kittens were not taken to the vet to be put down, but dumped unceremoniously in a bucket of water or swill, and held down until they drowned. This inhuman practice was only one of many thoughtless acts in farming that were born of expediency and practicality, not of cruelty. It was just the way it was and had been, and no one thought that it should change. Somehow, Toots had defied his fate and escaped, only to find himself alone and apparently destined to starve. I rescued him, saved his life and he was grateful to his dying day. We became almost inseparable. He followed me around the farm and, when I walked home from school, I would find him waiting for me in the hedgerow, some distance from the farm. He sat on my shoulder at meal-times and on my lap by the fireside. He was cuddled, coddled and fussed over and he responded with love and multiple presents of dead mice.

Farming in West Wales between the wars was hard. Much of the land was poor and, to compound the problem, many farmers were either too poor to replenish lost soil fertility, or they were ignorant of good husbandry. There were some farms that were well-managed and the farmers reasonably affluent, but on the smaller farms, and where farming practice was primitive, there was grinding poverty. Yet no one died of starvation, as they did in the mining valleys and in the towns. A farming community will always feed itself. In summer there were ample supplies of fruits and vegetables, both wild and cultivated, and surplus produce was preserved for consumption in the lean months. In spring and summer our hens laid enough eggs to feed a small village. In winter they were less inclined to reproduce and egg production fell dramatically, so part of the summer surplus was pickled in a large earthen-ware cauldron of isinglass, and used in winter for cooking. The other part of the surplus, together with the butter we produced, became part of a bartering system. On Friday evenings a large van pulled up at the farm gate, and Mother and I carried baskets of our produce down to it, exchanging eggs and butter for tea, sugar, soap and whatever, to an equivalent value. If we were in luck, we might make a pound or two on the deal, but hard cash seldom changed hands in any quantity. Indeed, there were times when Jones the Van already had as many eggs as his town shop could possibly sell. Kind and generous though he was, he was 'egg-bound' and could take no more, so our surplus was fed to the pigs. He sometimes offered us a penny a dozen for them and probably threw them away when he got back to base, such was his reluctance to say no.

On the poorer farmsteads, families subsisted on a basic diet of bread, home-cured bacon, eggs, potatoes, home-made jam and butter, if it hadn't all been sold or bartered. With no money coming in, their greatest problem was clothing. The signs were obvious. It could be that the children stopped coming to school because their footwear, dresses or trousers were too threadbare to merit inspection, let alone keep out the cold. The word went around and parcels of cast-off clothing and other necessities would find their way to the needy and be received with gratitude and without embarrassment.

In fact, every farm, every person, was a vital cog in the wheel of a community that could not have survived without the contribution of its constituent parts; we, at Ty-Cornel, were a segment of the whole. The farming system was based on communal co-operation in an age when horse-power meant what it implied. The tractor had not extended its clamorous pollution to the far west and we relied entirely on the horse.

Our small farm was one of six or seven, each with a farming capacity of between ten and fifteen acres. Placed roughly in the centre of our circle of smallholdings stood a larger farm of about sixty acres, which was equipped with all the necessary

farming implements that, for the smallholders, were unec-
onomical to own, assuming that they were affordable. Our
pivot was Griffiths, Penlan Farm, whose outbuildings housed
two horses, two carts, a hay-cutting machine, a hay-rake and
the forerunner of the combine-harvester – a corn-binder. The
hay harvest began in June and spread over a period of about six
weeks, weather permitting. We and our fellow smallholders
consulted with Griffiths, and worked out a rota system to
decide when it was convenient for him to bring his various
machines and horses to cut and bring in our hay. In return, we
provided the concentrated manpower (and womanpower) to
harvest his hay crop. In the absence of telephones, our inter-
farm communications system was primitive, effective and cost
nothing. When Penlan's hay needed our presence, Mrs Griffiths hung a white bedsheet out of an upstairs window. It
would be seen by neighbouring smallholders, the word was
passed round and within the hour a clutch of at least eight
men and three or four women reported for duty in Penlan's
farmyard. The cut swathes of hay were left to lie in the sun for
a day or two, then turned by hand-rake. When the lower
surface was dry and 'cured', the hay was lifted and shaken,
either by hand or machine, to aerate and thoroughly dry it.
Finally, when the grass had lost its sap and changed colour
from a glistening green to a desiccated greenish-brown, it was
deemed fit for stacking.

Diwrnod Y Gwair (the hay day) was a festive occasion,
despite the hard labour involved – and hard it was. Having
been machine-raked into dense rows, the hay was heaved on
to a cart by pitchfork. The overall weight of hay had to be
evenly apportioned, or else the whole load capsized on its
way to the farmyard. As the men pitched and the cart rolled
forward, the women followed, raking up every wisp of hay
into small mounds. Nothing was wasted. The presence of the
women also acted as a catalyst. The men in their braces and
flannel shirts strove to outwork each other, and there was
much banter and leg-pulling, which all contributed to a sense
of celebration.

At the farmyard, the laden carts were tipped and the hay pitchforked on to a hayrick, built on a foundation of logs and branches. The task of its construction was always consigned to an expert, and the finished product was a model of perfection, with vertical sides and a gently sloping 'roof', which was left to consolidate for a few weeks and then thatched with reeds or straw, to keep the hay dry. Large farms had a distinct advantage over the smallholdings. They possessed covered haybarns which made rick construction very much easier and quicker, and the hay was hoisted mechanically by horse-power.

Until I was old enough and strong enough to qualify as a pitchforker, it was my job to lead the horse backwards and forwards ad infinitum, until the last load was in, or the evening dew prevented further harvesting. I quite enjoyed the toing and froing and working with the wonderfully gentle farm-horses, as long as their heavy hooves didn't land on my fragile feet, which they did at times when my concentration strayed. For me, the best part of haymaking came at the end of the day, when the work was done. As dusk fell, we all gathered in the farmyard and sat on logs, bits of machinery or on the ground. When everyone was present, the women emerged from the house, bearing basins which they filled with sweet, piping-hot tea. Then came heaped plates of oven-baked bread, sliced and thickly buttered and filled with generous wedges of home-cured ham and accompanied by steaming bowls of new potatoes, freshly dug from the garden. We were ravenous, devoured the lot in double-quick time and, with sighs of contentment and a few belches, the men eased their tired limbs, lit their pipes and Woodbines and began to reminisce on seasons past, spiced with local gossip. 'Did you know that ... had a baby last week and she was only married two months ago?' 'Ah,' rejoined a well-known wag, 'speed is everything nowadays!' Another rotund and bearded character made the following mysterious pronouncement: 'If yesterday was today and today was yesterday, my hay would be like sniff'. We all fell silent and I'm still trying to work that one out. As the light faded and the early moon stood sentry for the sun, I mounted my bike and rode home to bed and another day, another hay at another farm.

The 'day of the bicycle' is also etched deep in my memory. By a stroke of luck and pure coincidence, Dad was home and it was my tenth birthday, on a Saturday. After breakfast Dad announced that he was going to the nearby village, a mile distant, and asked me to go with him. When we got there, he made a beeline for the clog-makers' shack. They were father and son, and behind their workshop stood another shack where a second son plied his trade as bicycle dealer and repairer. It was there I was led, to be greeted by my birthday present – a brand-new, shining Hercules bicycle, complete with bell and battery lamp. I was speechless, consumed with joy and gratitude, and my pleasure was reflected in my father's eyes and smile. That wonderful velocipede cost the princely sum of £3. 19s. 6d. (more or less £4.00 in today's devalued currency), but to me it was priceless, beyond my wildest dreams. The time taken to go to school was more than halved, which meant that my morning chores could be completed at a more leisurely pace and I could take more time over my breakfast.

By present day standards and teaching, my first meal of the day back in the 1930s was a death sentence. In summer it consisted of two eggs, slices of fatty, salty home-cured bacon and a mini-mountain of thickly buttered wholemeal bread. In winter, when eggs were fewer and sold at a good price, my deep plate was filled with hot, liquid bacon fat, into which I plopped drops of rich, brown HP sauce. Scooped up with bread and butter, it fuelled my youthful frame, and I thought it was the food of the gods. According to modern medical science, my breakfast contained enough fat and cholesterol to cripple an elephant, yet here am I, still relishing my food – although I have given up the lakes of bacon fat!

The corn harvest at Penlan farm was much less labour intensive than gleaning the hay crop. All it required was two men, two horses, the binder-machine and a cart. At Penlan, the binder presented a problem: it had to be drawn by two horses and the driver was seated some distance to their rear. They, the horses, were 'Bal' and 'Flower', mother and daughter respectively. Bal was a conscientious creature and once in the shafts she more than pulled her weight. Flower was a crafty young devil. She quickly learnt that the driver had his hands full, manipulating the unwieldy machine, and that he was too far back to cause her actual bodily harm, so she 'swung the lead', to use an army phrase. She dawdled whilst Bal strove, which was grossly unfair on the older mare. The solution to the dilemma was to have me astride Flower, armed with a slip of a cane, to encourage her when she slackened her stride. It may seem an easy job and it was, except for one drawback: sitting astride a sweating horse on a hot summer's day plays havoc with one's nether regions, and there were evenings when I rode home on my bike without my posterior touching the saddle once.

Grandmother's cure for inflamed flesh was goose grease liberally applied to the affected parts, and it worked wonders. She had many other basic remedies as well. For a sore throat, I was sent to bed with a chunk of warm pig's lard around my neck, held in place by one of my socks and a safety pin. The cure for earache was even more primitive. A thimbleful of my own warm pee was poured into my earhole and stoppered with a plug of cotton wool. All the treatments were very efficacious and maybe I own my continued good health to the unlikely combination of Syrup of Figs, senna pods, goose grease, pig's lard and urine!

Among our few neighbours were a Mr and Mrs Beynon, who had taken up rented residence in the thatched lodge of Tyllwyd mansion. Beynon had been a coal miner in one of the South Wales valleys, until the depression closed the pit and he and his wife had come westward to find work and refuge. He was a strong and steady worker and soon found casual work around the farms. He worked at least once a week for us, being paid 2 shillings (10 pence) a day, plus a cooked lunch, and often Mother gave him a bonus of a packet of ten Woodbines, price fourpence (1.7 pence). In stark contrast to a daily journey from the sun to the black seam of coal, he viewed his new life above ground with zest and pleasure. The only cloud on his otherwise clear horizon was Mrs Beynon. She was kinder to her cat than to her husband, yet she and I got on well together. She was built like a beanpole, without a single bump or curve to profess her femininity. Her hair was jet-black, dead straight and she cut it herself, using an upturned basin to guide her scissor-held hands. She was also endowed with supernatural powers and foretold the future with unnerving accuracy for half-a-crown ($12\frac{1}{2}$ pence) a sitting.

I delivered this odd couple their daily milk and once, and only once, Mrs Beynon invited me to sit while she told my fortune free of charge. A pack of playing cards was produced, which I was told to shuffle and hand back to her. She then laid a number of the top cards face upwards on the table and studied them intently for several minutes, glancing in my direction from time to time. At the age of fourteen, I was told what the future held for me. I would travel far and wide, over the sea. I would meet danger and survive many perils. I would be wed before I was twenty-one and I would father two children. I thought she was off her rocker, but her eyes saw what mine were blind to. All her prophecies came true in the fullness of time, but more of that later.

In the late thirties there occurred an incident which I shall never forget. Mrs Beynon contracted cancer and took to her bed, accompanied by Twm the cat. She knew what ailed her and flatly refused medical attention. She stoically consigned herself to her fate and as the weeks passed she became increasingly thin and more haggard. She and her husband were not rich by any standards, but they were not paupers either. He earned a steady pound or so a week and, in those days, it was enough to live on and they lived frugally. They had a large vegetable garden and a few chickens to supplement Beynon's earnings, and she did well out of her fortune telling, especially in summer when the visitors came to enjoy the Cardiganshire coast.

I still delivered the milk and spent a few minutes by her bedside each day. And so it continued until the day I made my last delivery. I opened the door as usual and called out. There was no reply and when I peered into the bedroom, it was empty. I left the milk on the table and retraced my steps, to be met by Mrs Beynon coming from the direction of the garden. She appeared a ghostly figure, dressed from chin to toe in a long white flannel nightdress, with a white lace night-cap on her still tar-black hair. She walked erect and proud and bade me enter the house with her. From somewhere she produced a pound note, gave it to me, thanked me for my services over the years and said, 'Go now. We will not meet again in this life.' We didn't. She died in the night and left not a single penny. Beynon searched high and low, even higher and lower, but he never discovered what she had done with her assets. I have often wondered what she had been up to in the garden on her last day, but I never let on. She had sworn me to secrecy, and I have respected her confidence until now, when I feel that I am free at last to tell the tale.

Memories are fickle and fanciful, and the years may have coloured my image of the thirties, a time that I remember as a period of sunny, carefree summers. 1936 was certainly unfor-gettable. June was dry and the land shimmered under blue, cloudless skies. Hay crops were abundant and not a drop of rain fell to mar the harvest. We farmers rejoiced in Nature's bounty but, all too soon, our joy turned to premonitions of hard times ahead. The skies stayed cloudless, no rain came, and by August the fields and hedgerows were uniformly khaki-coloured. Cows had a lean and hungry look and milk production fell abysmally low.

Fortunately, one of our fields was boggy, and we sup-plemented the grazing with our newly-harvested hay, hoping that there would be enough in reserve to see the winter through. Water, or the lack of it, was our greatest problem. The spring went from a gush to a trickle and then dried up. We turned to the well and bucketed the water out for the cows, until that also petered out. We were left with but one source of the precious liquid – a tap in the wall by Tyllwyd Lodge, about 300 yards from our thirsty cows. There was only one way of conveying the water from tap to cow – someone had to carry it, and the someones were Mother and I. Every morning and evening we made at least one trip, carrying a full 2-gallon can in one hand and another four or five gallons in the zinc bath, between us. It was hard graft, and for the first time in my life I came to appreciate the value of the life-sustaining liquid we call water, which until then, I had taken for granted.

My learning process continued apace. In those days, sex education was not on any school curriculum. For youngsters who lived on a farm, there was no necessity to talk about the birds and the bees; it was happening all around us. By merely observing animal behaviour, I soon learnt the difference between males and females and, much later, came to appreciate the French phrase *vive la différence*. It was the cows that completed my sex education. When their 'time' came, the normally placid creatures became restless and mooed incessantly in loud, demanding bellows. Friesian always came to the farmyard gate and yelled her head off. Her intended spouse, a huge bull of the same breed, lived on a farm two miles distant, and it was my duty to present Friesian's hoof in marriage to the handsome beast. She knew the drill down to the last detail. I'd place a rope halter round her neck and off we'd go. She strode purposefully but peaceably, and only once did she let me down. We were about halfway to the betrothal when we rounded a corner and a large piece of white paper blew out of the hedge. Frightened out of her wits, Friesian took off. With the halter rope looped round my hand, I couldn't let go, even if I'd wanted to, and so we sped along, passing through the village of Croeswen at well above the speed limit. My feet hardly touched the ground until we reached our destination, but my troubles were not yet over. The whole episode had upset our Friesian. Gone was her burning passion, and when the bull was led out she went into top gear yet again. Together we cleared a low stone wall and ploughed through a morass of manure where, unfortunately, I lost my wellies. They stuck fast, while I continued my headlong flight. I was really attached to the cow! She eventually came to rest, and an hour or so later decided that, having come thus far, she might as well do what she came for and she did. Later we ambled home at a leisurely pace, she with a look of bovine bliss on her face and I with relief and sore feet. With our four cows, I made the 'bull-run' four times a year and was left in no doubt that Nature has wondrous ways.

My links and involvement with the chapel not only continued, but were consolidated after our move to Ty-Cornel. Our nearest place of worship was in the village of Beulah about two miles away and, until my bicycle arrived, Mother and I made the journey there and back on foot, thrice a Sunday on average. Grandmother was too fragile to face the four-mile round trip but, fortunately, our minister, Tegryn Davies, moved to live in Aberporth, acquired an Austin 7 and, as he passed our door on his way to publicly forgive us our sins, he collected Mam and Grandma and returned them afterwards, penitent and purified. If my memory serves me right, his was the only car in Beulah on Sundays. Every other chapel-goer either walked, or came by pony and trap. On arrival, the pony was unhitched and housed in custom-built stables adjacent to the chapel vestry, and rehitched to the trap for the homeward journey.

We were allotted a pew immediately below the pulpit and to one side of it. This meant that we were in full, semi-frontal view of the whole congregation, which was a positive disadvantage. We had to appear to listen intently to the sermon which, more often than not, was as dry as a Non-Conformist was supposed to be. In fact, our lady organist fell into a deep sleep between every hymn, but she was forgiven because it was understood that she suffered from some obscure affliction or other. According to our chapel teaching, strong drink was an accursed beverage that led its imbibers on to the prickly path to hell. Temperance was preached from every pulpit and every youngster had to sign the pledge. It was an effective discipline, tinged with hypocrisy. Within a short distance of Ty-Cornel was The Gogerddan Arms, a Buckley's house run by a kindly, matronly widow woman and her daughter. Trade was brisk, yet I never saw a single soul enter or leave by the front door. Even the deacons lapsed once a year on the occasion of the annual Sunday School trip. The event was primarily for the children, but many adults, including the deacons, joined in. A few parents were essential, to maintain a semblance of order, and the deacons had a duty to perform. We never went very far, about five miles at most, to one of the lovely, sandy beaches nearby, but distance was immaterial. What mattered was a day out as a fraternity, to paddle, swim, build sand-castles and stuff ourselves with sandwiches, cake and pop. For the grown-ups, cups of tea were as vital as the Celtic blood in their veins. On arrival at the beach a delegation of deacons set-to to light a fire fuelled by the wood that, like the rest of us, had come on the bus. When there was a good head of flame, the deacons sallied forth in search of water which – surprise, surprise – could be divined only from The Ship Inn. Filling cans and buckets of water took a long time but, at last, a dawdle of deacons trooped down the hill, red of face, weighed down with water, sprightly of step and 'bitter-sweet' with happiness. It was truly a great day out, made even greater for many because it was their annual holiday. They were tied to their homes and farms for the remaining 364 days of the year.

In the days before radio and television intruded into our lives we made our own fun, and most of it radiated from the chapel – the hub of the community. There were regular prayer meetings, bible studies and concerts that were instrumental in preparing young children to face the larger world outside their parochial domain. We performed short, one-act plays, recited poetry or sang traditional Welsh songs, composed for the very young. For most of us, it was superb training that sowed the seeds of confidence. Some were less fortunate. It was every parent's ambition and pride to see their little Berian or Bronwen on the stage in front of an audience but, unfor-tunately, many B and Bs were ill-equipped to be budding

Burtons. They forgot their well-rehearsed lines and some were such a knot of nerves that, when they left the stage, a small wet pool marked the spot where they had stood.

In common with the Church of England and later, the Church in Wales, the chapel celebrated the Christian festivals in the normal way, with one exception. At Easter the men prepared for the *pwnc*, a word and a practice that has no equivalent in any other language, as far as I know. A chapter was chosen from the Bible by the minister, the men assembled together in a body in the centre pews and co-recited the verses in a monotonic staccato fashion, with abrupt pauses at every comma, colon and full stop. I found the whole thing amusing, fruitless and by no means worshipful. For some reason, I compared it to a herd of bison smitten with spasmodic cramp!

The chapel also had close links with the *eisteddfod*, an event best defined as a competitive concert for voices and instruments, mainly for voices. Competitions were divided into age groups, starting with the youngest and ascending to minds and voices in their prime and beyond to the 'a bit past its' with a hymn singing competition of their own. There were solo competitions for all voices, recitations, pianoforte duels, and competitions for poets who fancied their chances at composing eternal masterpieces of poetry and prose. Many of the *eisteddfodau* were held in the local chapel. The action began at about 2 p.m. and it was often well past midnight before the Champion Solo competition ended and a proud soprano or baritone walked off with the cup and a pound note for endurance and a God-given voice. The solo winners were our heroes. We accorded them the deference and idolatry that today's footballers, boxers and tennis players command from their fans. If they could afford the time, the effort and the money, the local stars went on to compete at regional *eisteddfodau* and then, wonder of wonders,The Royal National *Eisteddfod* of Wales. Those that actually won at *Y Genedlaethol* (The National) came home as kings. We lesser mortals were proud to touch the hem of their garments and they were revered for evermore in the temples of Welsh talent.

The chapel did all these things. It also baptised, married and buried its members with dignity and discipline. It gathered the fragmented community comfortably within its creeds, and its security embraced all ages and all walks of life. It preached independence, generosity and kindness, yet it could be cold and cruel in pursuit of its dogmas. Premarital sex was deemed sinful, yet strangely tolerated, providing it was discreet; but premarital pregnancy was unforgivable, albeit accidental. At a time in her young life when a girl needed support, when the hand of help and guidance should have been extended, the chapel heartlessly denounced her. She was brought before the congregation at a Sunday service and publicly condemned for her deeds from the pulpit and cast out, never to darken the chapel's doors again. The man, the father, got away unpunished although his identity was usually known to all and sundry. After I saw it happen, the words 'and forgive us our trespasses, as we forgive them that trespass against us', rang false against the chapel walls that reputedly housed us Christians, the children of a forgiving God.

Some time in the mid-thirties the family took the first fateful step towards modernisation – Father bought a wireless. I can see it now: the working parts were contained in a box, the size and appearance of a small coffin. At the front were two large black dials and, inside, a ravel of wires wound their way around valves, condensers and who knows what, together with what looked like two large reels of green thread, and on the 'coffin' lid sat a massive ear trumpet. It had to be at full volume, and even then reception was little more than a whisper. The ladies were not impressed by the new contraption, and in Dad's absence I was the 'coffin's' only customer. In winter I wore an overcoat and gloves to listen to my favourite comedians, Clapham and Dwyer, Nosmo King, The Two Leslies and Flanagan and Allen. The wireless was in the sitting-room, the fire was in the kitchen, so I took my entertainment in icy, solitary state. To change wavelength one had to move the ear-trumpet, open the lid and do a flick over from one green 'cotton-reel' to the other. The whole caboodle was powered by a wet battery: a cumbersome, heavy glass contrivance that housed two metal plates and a quantity of sulphuric acid. When the power was spent, it was up to me to take the battery on my bike to an enterprising chap with a windmill in his backyard. The windmill provided the power that recharged the battery, so the time taken to pump life into it was entirely dependent on the velocity and frequency of the air currents in the vicinity of Beulah village. Still, it only cost sixpence ($2\frac{1}{2}$ pence) and we carried a spare wet battery as a cover against periods of calm weather. It was on that primitive, temperamental set that I heard the historic battle between the great boxers Tommy Farr of Tonypandy and the American Joe Louis. The fight went the full fifteen rounds and Louis got the verdict, but it was our Tommy who won, as any Welshman will tell you. The whole nation was in the ring with Farr that night and I was actually permitted to stay up and listen to the contest, broadcast at around 2 a.m. I had to practically stick my head in the speaker to hear the fight commentary, it was so faint. Well, it would be, wouldn't it? New York was a world away from Ty-Cornel.

It was about this time that my trusty Hercules expired from acute metal fatigue and I was given a new bike. It was a drop-handlebar Sturmey-Archer 3-speed, Raleigh, and from my own pocket money I added the final touch – a gleaming chromium-plated acetylene lamp. I was the envy of the lads for miles around. The lamp emitted a wide beam of white light, providing I remembered to feed it. There were two com-partments, one above the other. The bottom one held dry calcium carbide and the top one, water. By turning a threaded switch, water and carbide met, a chemical action ensued and a gaseous stench was emitted. It emerged through a jet in front of the reflector and, at the touch of a lighted match, it burst into flame. Maintenance entailed 'Silvo-ing' the chrome, clean-ing the jet and keeping the two compartments charged with the essential materials. There was little, or no, crime in those days, so the local constabulary sought out drunks and cyclists with no front and rear lights at night. Failure to illuminate one's progress resulted in a five-shilling (25 pence) fine and to be branded a criminal in the local paper, the *Cardigan and Tivyside Advertiser*. I made every effort to keep my lamp fully charged, especially the carbide compartment, because, if the carbide became exhausted on a long journey, it could not be replaced, but water replenishment was no problem – I always carried my own!

It was during this period that my father met with an experience that shook him to the core. The Spanish Civil War was in full swing and his ship, along with others, ran the blockade to off-load supplies of much-needed coal to Spanish ports. The ship made several such voyages until it finally met its fate. Whilst in dock in Barcelona, it was dive-bombed and rendered unseaworthy but, fortunately, all the crew survived. We knew nothing of these events at home, which was just as well, otherwise we would have been desperately worried. I remember Father's homecoming vividly. At around 8.30 a.m. I was walking to catch the school bus when the mail van approached and, to my astonishment, disgorged my father, clutching a paper parcel. His clothes looked as though he had slept in them (which he had) and he sported a seven o'clock shadow that had seen several days' growth. We exchanged bear-like hugs and he bade me continue on my journey to school. All I know of his experiences is that he escaped injury and somehow managed to return home via France, to end his journey by hitching a lift for the last seven miles in a GPO van. He never talked of his trials and tribulations and on the only occasion I plied him with questions, he replied, 'It's best not to talk about it,' and I respected his wishes. That's the kind of man he was; but he never set sail in another ship again.

1935 was another milestone in my academic progress – I sat the Scholarship, which in due course became the Eleven Plus. With eight other pupils from Glynarthen school and between 150 and 200 other quaking young hopefuls, I reported to Cardigan County Grammar School and sat two test papers. To everyone's surprise, and not least to my own, I came eighth and realised that I had a brain somewhere between my ears.

The complement of each form at the grammar school varied between thirty and thirty-five pupils and I can honestly write that each and every one had a fair deal. The teaching staff were well qualified in their subjects, they were dedicated to their chosen profession and, with one or two exceptions, they were kind, considerate and patient. Furthermore, theirs wasn't a nine till four job. We received extra-curricular instruction in the sport of our choice – tennis, cricket, or swimming in summer, and in winter, either hockey or rugby.

The headmaster was a kindly soul, subject to fits of rabid rage. He had been christened Thomas Evans, but was known to us all as '*Twm* Pop'. It so happened that Corona, the most popular cordial of the time, was manufactured by the firm of Thomas & Evans, so it was only natural that our Head became '*Twm* Pop', just as very many years later, Sir David Maxwell Fyfe became '*Dai* Bananas' on his appointment as Welsh Secretary.

Smoking was strictly forbidden in school, although *Twm* himself got through forty Craven A a day, and the staff room was enveloped in a blue smog during breaks. By the age of thirteen I had become wedded to the Woodbine and, together with my fellow miscreants, we sneaked a quick 'drag' in the 'lavs' at break-times. My pocket money was the princely sum of one shilling (5 pence) per week and I could buy my Woodbines at two a penny (less than a $\frac{1}{2}$ pence) from a shop near the school. Inevitably, I was caught smoking more than once, marched to the Head's study and subjected to six of the best, applied either on the hands, or on the posterior. We dared not tell our parents when this happened, because we would have received no sympathy from them.

It was also a highly competitive society from the moment we attended school. There were tests at the close of each term and a more detailed exam at the end of the school year. We took our school reports home with varying degrees of pride or apprehension and, although my position in the class was usually in the top ten, the words 'could do better' and 'easily distracted' appeared all too often. We competed on the sports-

field also. One of my proudest moments came when the *Wyddfa*
House captain selected me for his rugby team, as a prop
forward. I nearly burst my buttons when I was picked to play
for the school, and I wore the school jersey with immense
pride.

One of the highlights of the year was the school opera,
performed for three nights on the stage of the town's cinema.
We played to full houses, comprised mainly of proud parents,
aunts and uncles who came along to watch their young rela-
tives perform. In my time we staged, *Il Trovatore*, *The Gondoliers*,
The Pirates of Penzance and *The Mikado*. In *Il Trovatore* I was a
spear-carrying soldier, and one of the able-bodied seamen in
The Pirates. Then came success! In *The Gondoliers* I was singled
out from the other boat pushers and given a speaking part. At
a critical point in the performance I stepped forward from the
chorusline and, in ringing tones, asked, 'For whom prepare ye
these floral tributes extraordinary?' It was a tough baptism!
The principal parts in the operas were allotted to recognised,
adult local singers, some of whom had won acclaim on the
national stage. By the time we did *The Mikado* I was seventeen,
and my voice had matured into a 'rich, melodious baritone',
so melodious that I was invited to join the lead singers and
given the part of the Lord Pish Tush. I sang it and gave it
everything I'd got, convinced that this was the first step to
standing ovations at La Scala, Milan and the other great opera
houses of the world. In fact, I did receive an offer to join the
D'Oyly Carte Company, but alas it was not to be. Mother
considered the stage to be a den of iniquity, not worthy of her
young and innocent son!

Towards the end of the thirties in our far corner of Wales, I
was vaguely aware of unrest on the Continent, and the names
of Adolf Hitler and Benito Mussolini crept into conversation.
Life went serenely on. I didn't imagine for a moment that the
prattlings and posturings of these rather comic figures could
possibly affect my untroubled life. The Prime Minister, Neville
Chamberlain, flew home from Munich, and descended the

steps of the plane waving a piece of paper, declaring 'peace in our time'. Then war broke out.

On the third of September 1939, the day war was declared, I was spending a final week's holiday with an aunt in Cardiff and, early on the fateful evening, we had gone to one of the city's cinemas. When we emerged, the city was in total darkness, my aunt walked smack into a pillar-box and we experienced our first 'black-out', a precaution that was to last for nearly six years. Headlights on all vehicles were fitted with special adaptors that directed light downwards so that it could not be detected from the air. Houses, offices and factories were blacked out and air-raid wardens patrolled the streets, pouncing on the faintest glimmer of light. They were black days indeed, and became blacker with the passing years, although in the West Walian farming community we suffered but lightly. We escaped the bombing and, although food rationing was universal, we enjoyed an infinitely better and more varied diet than the people in the towns and cities. Our milk was sold in bulk in churns and was collected daily by lorry, but we were allowed to retain enough to make a pound or two of butter for our own consumption. We were permitted to keep and slaughter one, and only one, pig, and we kept enough eggs to feed ourselves. Clothing, petrol, furniture, sugar, cheese, jam and many other commodities were strictly rationed; things like tinned fruit, oranges and bananas vanished completely from the shops. In summer every family was allocated extra sugar for jam-making. We tightened our belts a bit and, in Cardiganshire, carried on much as before.

As time passed, we heard and read news of the German bombing of London and other cities and ports. I well remember the night Swansea got a hammering. Wave after wave of bombers came, dropped their deadly cargo and laid waste the town centre. I was cycling home at the time, and the far horizon, some forty miles away, was lit as bright as day, while Swansea burned and people perished. I was too far distant to appreciate the sheer horror and futility of it all; that was to come later.

In the seaside fishing village of Aberporth, premonitions of change came upon the backwater inhabitants some time prior to the outbreak of hostilities. On the high ground above the cliffs, a large establishment was in the process of being built. It provided much-needed work for the local populace and, in due course, it became the PDE – Projectile Development Establishment. Two miles inland, several farm acres were compulsorily purchased and an aerodrome mushroomed into being. The farmer steadfastly refused to abandon his home and, to this day, his family farm the remaining acres with the Royal Air Force in close attendance. The population of Aberporth increased almost overnight, and the once tranquil, secluded village was changed for all time. No one knew for sure what went on at the PDE or at the aerodrome. Everything was shrouded in secrecy. But it was obvious, even to the dimwitted, that the unaccustomed activity on the headland had military connotations. The peace of the village was shattered almost daily as artillery gunfire belched from the clifftops, aimed at a lone biplane with a large target in tow. Occasionally, small, silken parachutes drifted in from the sea and came down in the village. With clothes rationing beginning to bite, they vanished as soon as they came to earth, and the village ladies wore parachute knickers of the finest silk.

Over in France the British and German armies faced each other from their entrenched and fortified positions in the Maginot and Siegfried lines respectively. Displaying superb strategy, the German Panzer tank divisions bypassed the fortifications. We heard the news on the radio and, as the days passed, the tidings from across the Channel became progressively worse. The British Expeditionary Force was in retreat to Dunkirk. Many of the war-ravaged soldiers were rescued and transported to Aberporth, to recover and recuperate from their mental and physical wounds. For the first time, the realities of cruel conflict were brought home to us.

As the bombing of London and other major cities increased in intensity, the Government came to the reluctant but wise decision to evacuate children to safer havens. So it was that on a black winter's night, a car drew up at our gate and set down our very own London evacuee. Her name was Jean and she came from Willesden. Clad only in a vest, pants, shoes, ankle-socks and a thin cotton dress, she cut a pathetic, shivering figure by the light of the paraffin lamp in our Welsh kitchen. She was five years old, her eyes showed fear and trepidation, and my heart went out to her. Being a practical soul, Mother listed her priorities. First and foremost our waif and stray had to be cleaned and her hair examined for foreign bodies. The zinc bath was brought out, half filled with warm water, and Jean was told to strip off and to stand in it. Her city-white skin covering her painfully thin, fragile body was soaped, flannelled, re-soaped and washed down, until every atom of grime had been removed. Her hair was de-bugged, she was dressed in clean clothing borrowed from my sister, fed and put into the bed she was to share with my sister for several years. And she cried herself to sleep. With the resilience of youth, however, she soon settled down, and I became her big-brother hero. She had the appetite of a ravenous barracuda and ate everything placed before her with obvious enjoyment. We learnt from her that her staple diet at home had been very, very basic – bread, jam and chips and apparently little else. In her first summer Jean was a constant source of amusement and revelation. She enjoyed the fresh vegetables from the garden and her first ever taste of freshly-dug new potatoes was pure ecstasy. After the first tentative mouthful, she ate and ate until her distended 'tum' could accommodate no more. It was the first and only time that I have ever seen a human being so full of food that her eyes stood out like organ stops!

Coming from the bricks and concrete of the London area, the countryside was a new and exciting experience for our little evacuee. When I was home, she followed me everywhere and in a strange way she opened my eyes to many of Nature's marvels that I had missed. She was an intelligent little thing with a thirst for knowledge, and her constant questioning made me realise how little I knew of the land and its flora and fauna. To quench her thirst for information, I bought books on insects and wild flowers, and together we learnt their names and habits. I left home in 1942 and by the time I returned, four years later, Jean was back with her parents in London. We had no forwarding address and contact was lost. I still wonder at times what became of my little friend.

The year of Our Lord 1940 fashioned my future in no uncertain terms. I was a mature seventeen-year-old and I had a steady girlfriend, mainly because most of my contemporaries sought the company of the fairer sex and I felt I should follow suit. I took her to the pictures and we exchanged grubby love-notes from time to time. It meant nothing but, nevertheless, I quite enjoyed her company. Our liaison came to an abrupt conclusion when, in common with many other local girls, she fell for a soldier's uniform. Within twenty-four hours she was but a memory, and then it happened. It was a Saturday morning and I was in school doing some extra work in the chemistry lab, and preparing to play rugby against an opposing school in the afternoon. My work done, I quit the lab, crossed the quad, and strode down a corridor. In front of me dawdled two damsels heading in the same direction and suddenly my world stood still. They were both comely creatures, but the one on the right was something special. From the rear she had it all! Long auburn hair tumbled about her ears, her figure would have given the Venus de Milo an inferiority complex, and her black-clad legs seemed endlessly shapely. I overtook the vision, turned and recognised her as a girl in Form 5A whom I'd known for years. Why hadn't I noticed her before? Was I blind to beauty? I don't know the answers, but what I did know was that I had stumbled upon my destiny. Without any words of preamble, I invited her to accompany me to the cinema that evening and, to my astonishment and delight Glenys accepted.

I played the game of my life that fateful afternoon and we won; the girls were also victorious in hockey. With Glen in the team, how could they fail? After the game we showered (separately, of course) and I walked my new-found love to the Pavilion. I bought two fourpenny (1½ pence) tickets, found two tip-up seats towards the rear of the house and we settled down to await the latest screen epic. The lights dimmed, were extinguished, and with beating heart and trepidation I put my arm around Glen's shoulders. There was a momentary spasm of stiffness and then, to my surprise and delight, she nestled closer. The action on the silver screen passed unnoticed by me and to this day I have no idea whether the film was a tear-jerker, or a bloodthirsty western. For the first time in my young life, I was hopelessly, irretrievably and permanently in love. I must have known, even then, that here was the girl that I wanted to be at my side throughout life's journey.

Glen was also unwittingly responsible for my first adult encounter with fear and abject despair. In school we sought each other's company at breaktimes, and at weekends and during the holidays we spent our time together, swimming and larking about on the beach in summer and walking the high-hedged, country lanes in winter. This lovely slip of a girl had become as essential to my living as the air I breathed. Then, one day she was absent from school. I assumed that she had been struck down with some bug or other, but it wasn't until I called at her home on my way home from school that I was made aware of the seriousness of the malady that had deprived me of her company. Out of nowhere and for no reason, she had contracted meningitis, a serious enough illness these days, but in those unenlightened times it was, all too often, fatal. On my visit the following evening I was allowed to see her. She lay comatose in her bed, her eyes closed, her breathing laboured and her temperature as high as any human body can withstand. With the recklessness and ignorance of youth, I bent and kissed her and for a fleeting moment her eyes flickered and a hint of a smile played on her fevered face, before she lapsed again into total unawareness. It was the first sign of life she had shown since the disease had laid her low and her mother believed that the brief moment of contact between Glen and I had somehow strengthened her will to fight her affliction. I don't know. Her miraculous recovery was more probably due to the best medical treatment in the land,

and by the then new drug M & B 693. I have no idea what those letters and figures signify; all I do know is that they battled the bacteria, won and gave me back the most precious being in my life.

Glen made a complete recovery. I spent as much time as I could by her bedside and it was during this period that I resolved that one day she would be my wife. It may be that seeing her in bed, adorned in her schoolgirl pyjamas, instilled visions of the future! I think it was more than that. Having contemplated an existence without her by my side, I was determined that all other males within an attainable radius should be made aware that Glen was 'spoken for'. I suggested that we should become engaged and she agreed without a moment's hesitation, and as tender teenagers, we pledged our troth.

Things were going well. The first hurdle in love's tempestuous path had been cleared with ease, but I knew that I had to consolidate my position as the front runner in the 'Glen stakes'. An engagement ring would seal our contract and our fate, and it would have to be a solitaire diamond. Only the best would do for my girl. My pocket money had risen to 2 shillings and sixpence ($12\frac{1}{2}$ pence) a week, but my running expenses left me penniless by the end of each week. As near as I can recall, my weekly budget was as follows:

Approx. 5 Woodbines a day	= 1/– (5p)
2 seats at the cinema	= 8d ($3\frac{1}{2}$p)
2 après cinema meals	= 1/– (5p)
Total	= 2/8 ($13\frac{1}{2}$p)

In other words, I was twopence (1 pence) over income and there was no way I could make up the deficit, except by reducing my Woodbine consumption. I insisted that I should pay for the cinema seats and for our meals in Volk's Café before boarding the last bus home. At sixpence ($2\frac{1}{2}$ pence) each, the meals were good value. For that princely sum we each had a plate of egg and chips, bread and butter and a cup of tea, and in winter a coal fire enhanced the glow of true love on our faces. What is more, the room was usually empty and we could indulge in a kiss and a cuddle before venturing forth to face an ever curious public.

However, my overspending was not a problem. Meat was rigorously rationed, with just about enough ration coupons to provide a family with sufficient for a single meal per week, with one exception. Farmland was overrun with rabbits, and there was no restriction on their capture and consumption. The rabbit population had to be controlled in the interest of grass and grain production, and so the farmers called in free-lance trappers, who employed iron-jawed gin-traps. The unfortunate rabbit was caught by one leg in a vicious, painful grip. It was a callous and cruel method of capture that is, thankfully, now illegal, but in those days it was accepted practice and no one gave it a second thought. With rabbits fetching sixpence ($2\frac{1}{2}$ pence) each, I acquired half a dozen gin-traps and, to my lasting shame, joined in the barbaric butchery. It is the only time in my life that I have inflicted cruelty on my fellow animals and my thoughtless deeds still trouble me. However, they did enable me to buy Glen the ring, which she wore on a ribbon around her neck, concealed from prying eyes, and our secret was safe.

In early 1940s the war was going very badly for Britain. We were deeply concerned with the conflict on our very doorstep and with the threat that our fair land was in danger of invasion by a ruthless enemy. As early as 1939, a civilian army known as the LDV (Local Defence Volunteers) had been formed. It was manned mainly by men in reserved occupations and those who were over-age for military service. Within a few months this volunteer rabble began to look as though it meant business. The men were issued with uniforms, Lee Enfield rifles, Bren and Tommy guns, and all the other paraphernalia that transforms an amorphous body of men into a fighting force, and they were re-christened the Home Guard. Much against my mother's wishes, I joined them, and began my short career as a soldier.

By and large, the Home Guard soon matured into a formidable defensive force. We received training in unarmed combat, arms drill, use of weapons including bayonet practice, explosives and Morse code signalling using flags, lamps and keys. There were weekend manoeuvres, where we attacked an imaginary enemy up mountains, across open country and defended coastal villages from possible maritime invasions. The training was comprehensive and of a high order, and it stood youngsters like myself in good stead when the time came for us to join the real army of regular soldiers and conscripts.

At the age of seventeen I received my first promotion to lance-corporal and wore the single stripe on my sleeve. A second stripe soon followed and then a third and I was appointed sergeant in charge of the school's army cadets. One of my proudest moment was marching through the town of Cardigan at the head of our Company. I trained and qualified as a signaller and, together with a Home Guard captain (a member of the school staff), toured the villages of South Cardiganshire, instructing the local Home Guard in signalling procedures. All this extra-curricular activity played the very devil with my love-life and with my studies, with the result that I failed all three subjects in the Central Welsh Board Higher Certificate examinations – and it didn't seem to matter one bit. There was a war on and subconsciously I knew that my future was 'on hold', awaiting developments; they were not long in coming.

In August 1942 the school cadet force set off for a week's training camp at Saundersfoot on the South Pembrokeshire coast. On the third day I received an official-looking brown envelope that had been forwarded from home. It contained an invitation from the reigning monarch, King George the Sixth, to join his army, promising free accommodation, food and clothing, with the possibility of all expenses paid overseas travel! How could I refuse?

That brown envelope contained much more than my call-up papers. It meant the end of the gentle, unhurried, carefree and secure life that had been mine for eighteen years. It severed me from the protective cocoon of a happy family life, from the people, plants and animals that I loved dearly and, worst of all, from Glen. Clad in my Home Guard uniform, I bade the family farewell on the morning of the third of September 1942. Glen and I travelled by bus to Cardigan and spent a few hours together, walking the lanes we knew so well. With heavy hearts, we dragged our feet to the station and at around 6 p.m. I boarded a train and in an agony of sadness we kissed goodbye, and then I was on my way to a strange and perilous new life.

In Uniform

✤

EVEN in wartime the Army's ways were wondrous and
mysterious. In 1942 there were three Welsh Regiments –
The South Wales Borderers, The Welch and The Royal
Welch Fusiliers, and there were several recruit training units
within the Principality. I was a Welsh-speaking youngster, yet
my orders were to report to 14 GTC (General Training Corps)
in Bodmin in Cornwall. The train I had boarded in Cardigan
took me to Bristol, where my travel warrant bore instructions
to change for Bodmin. As the Great Western steam engine
thundered through the night, a lonely, forlorn lad stood in the
corridor, wondering what was in store at the journey's end. I
was to find out soon enough.

The train pulled into Bodmin station at about 7 a.m. and
disgorged a number of raw recruits. I was one of them, but all
my fellow travellers were in civvies whilst I wore my Home
Guard uniform, complete with the rank of sergeant. On the
platform stood a corporal, waiting to march us to the camp.
He was about to 'get us fell in' in a semblance of three ranks
when he spotted my three stripes. Technically, I outranked
him and for a few moments he was lost for words. We could
almost hear him thinking. At last he reached a decision, told
me to stand aside and ordered the others to fall in. Then he
asked, actually asked, me to follow up in the rear, and so the
'shambles' made its way up to Bodmin barracks.

On arrival at the barrack square, we were allotted a hut, told
to dump our gear and report back immediately to be marched
to the cookhouse for breakfast. We queued for a plateful of

tepid, lumpy porridge, a mug of muddy tea and two sausages. The skins could have been fashioned from reject bicycle tyres and their innards were appropriately khaki-coloured and seemingly flavoured with essence of old socks. I was famished and managed to down the tea and porridge, but the bangers were beyond me. So ended my first army meal. Fortunately, our other meals in the camp were considerably better.

The hut that was destined to be our abode for the six-week training period held thirty assorted 'bods'. Most of us were eighteen-year-olds who had been called up as soon as we became of age. There were four Welshmen – three northerners from Caernarfonshire and me from Cardiganshire. It was natural that we should gravitate into a group and our few square feet of hut were designated 'Chinese Corner' by our fellows. The camp stood on a hillside overlooking the town and our accommodation consisted of the bare necessities and no more. The previous afternoon we had been issued with a mess tin, knife, fork and spoon, two pairs of boots, two sets of uniform and underwear, including, 'underpants, cellular, soldiers-for-the-use-of' and a wallet containing our toiletries. We were issued with two denim uniforms for use in field training, and two sets of serge uniforms for 'square-bashing' (drill), or 'walking out' and they, at times, caused us acute embarrassment. To prevent infestation by bugs in store, they had been dusted with some chlorinated powder. As long as the uniforms remained dry, all was well; we soon discovered that it was wise to keep them dry. On one occasion my friend and I walked from the camp to the local cinema and it rained *en route*. We bought our tickets, took our seats and in the cinema's warmth we began to smell like a chlorinated swimming-pool.

The training schedule was rigorous. For the first four of our six weeks' training we were all confined to camp, on the premise that we were unfit to be seen in public until we could walk out looking passably like smart and upright trained soldiers. The period of confinement was the most miserable of my whole existence. I missed my Glen, the family, the farm, the freedom and all the things that I'd grown to love and cherish. In their place were alien surroundings, strange faces and a loss of freedom that I found hard to tolerate. I began to live again when we were granted permission to leave camp from 14.00 hours to 22.00 hours on the fourth Saturday of our 'imprisonment'. Our platoon sergeant warned us that we would be inspected by the Regimental Sergeant Major at the guard-room gate. The fearsome figure of the RSM emerged, walked slowly round me three times, inspected my finger-nails, the undersides of my boots and my handkerchief. Then he asked to see my pay-book and 14270738 Private Clay-Jones had forgotten to put the darn thing in his pocket. I was ordered to fetch it, submitted to a brief reinspection and advised to conduct myself with due decorum among the Cornish public and to report back no later than 21.59 hours or else.

Once the transitory shock had passed, I took to soldiering with muted enthusiasm. I thoroughly enjoyed the field exercises and the route marches through the rugged and lovely Cornish countryside. Even arm drill instilled a sense of pride in our platoon, as we began to look more like soldiers and less like civilians in fancy dress. A few of our number found the harsh discipline difficult to swallow, but to me it seemed but a natural progression from the rules and regulations that had been my yardstick almost from birth.

The NCO (non-commissioned officer) instructors were exceptionally good and scrupulously fair. They laid the foundations of our survival in battle and were conscious of the heavy responsibility they bore. It is to their credit that, in the short space of forty-two days, they managed to transform a bunch of nondescript civilians into embryo soldiers. There is no doubt that in Bodmin I became a man. The carefree, opinionated and 'spoilt' youth who had walked in through the camp gates belonged to the past. In his place stood a figure, aware, for the first time, of the harsh reality of life.

And it was in Bodmin that I had my first taste of army medication. I awoke one morning with a raging toothache. I reported the fact to our platoon sergeant who, having established that I wasn't 'swinging the lead', but in real pain, bade me 'report sick'. I soon found myself in a dentist's chair in a hut that called itself the Dental Unit. The dentist was disconcertingly young and, having made a tentative inspection of my mouth, decreed that one of my molars was as rotten as sin and would have to come out. When he set about extracting the diseased tusk, the pain was excruciating. My molars have roots like parsnips and do not part readily from their niche in my jawbone. But he was a die-hard dentist who could have been a pneumatic drill operator in civilian life. He ended up with one knee on mine and the other on my chest until finally, with a cry of triumph, he fell to the floor, clutching my tooth in the jaws of his pincers. I bled all over him and made my escape. Feeling sorry for myself, I returned to our hut to find it empty, and sat on my bunk, nursing my aching jaw.

By an unfortunate twist of fate, that morning we were marched to the gas chamber and told to enter in groups of four, with the instructor in attendance. The exercise was intended to familiarise us with gas attack, and I suppose to prove beyond doubt that our gas masks were effective. To substantiate the claim, we were ordered to remove our gas masks in the gas-filled chamber for the space of a few seconds, presumably so that we could smell the vile stuff. From this pointless, futile exercise we emerged into the clean air coughing and spluttering and, in my case, with a wounded gum now aflame with searing pain. I expected no sympathy and got none. Training resumed as normal, the MO (Medical Officer) gave me some mouthwash and I healed. It was the army way. It was accepted, and the gas chamber exercise was but one of several manifestations of military futility that every serving man and woman experienced from time to time.

During the final week in Bodmin we were subjected to an intelligence test. According to our platoon sergeant, we were all a bunch of fatherless, idle morons and I suppose the test was meant to confirm his suspicions! I found the theory test so simple, it could have been completed by a moderately intelligent eleven year old. All one had to do, was to find the odd man out in several series of shapes, letters and figures. The practical test was another matter. By dint of deep concentration and much good fortune, I managed to reassemble the various pieces of everyday equipment, until I came to the final challenge – a completely disassembled mortice-lock. I put the thing together to the best of my ability and awaited the verdict of the examining officer with trepidation. All went well, until he came to the lock. He turned the key and the thing came to pieces – the spring shot across the room. The examiner said, 'Hmm.' Just that, but I never heard anyone put so much supercharged contempt into one syllable.

To clarify the next step in my army career, I must explain that, prior to our departure from Bodmin, we were all asked to state our regimental preferences. Being Welsh to my 'whatnots', I opted for the South Wales Borderers and became a private soldier in the Duke of Cornwall's Light Infantry! I was deeply disappointed. The SWBs were famed and feared among fighting men. They were the heroes of the Battle of Rorke's Drift, where their bravery in the face of overwhelming odds earned them seven Victoria Crosses. On the eleventh of January 1879, a battalion of SWBs faced 20,000 Zulu warriors. 1,329 brave Borderers lost their lives; there was no surrender. However, at least the DCLI was a Cornish regiment with strong Celtic connections, and I was resigned to my fate. I discovered that light infantry regiments were distinguished from other infantry outfits in two ways: they marched at a much faster pace, and they carried their rifles at the 'trail' position, horizontally, muzzle forward and with arms close to the sides. Although I never sought to reason why, I suspect it was because light infantry battalions travelled lightly equipped, in order to engage an enemy at short notice and prior to the arrival of the main force. We also wore green forage caps, in place of the khaki ones worn by other Welsh and English regiments. I exclude the Scots, whose headgear was both colourful and curious.

From Bodmin station we embarked for our various destinations, and I found myself alone in being posted for further training to the Goojerat Barracks in Colchester. The contrast in accommodation at Goojerat Barracks was startling. Colchester was a garrison town that housed troops in peace and war. In place of Bodmin's outside garden sheds were permanent brick buildings and an aura of stability. Along with twenty or so other members of our intake from other training units, we were shown to our barrack room. It was stoutly built, draught-proof, and the palliasses were fairly well padded with clean straw. But there were no beds or bunks, so on that first night we all slept on our strands of straw on a concrete floor. The reveille bugle roused us from slumber at 06.00 hours. I sat up, or tried to, and fell back in agony on to my palliasse – it was the dreaded lumbago that has smitten me from time to time over the years. I was immobile, locked in pain that only time and rest would alleviate. The corporal in charge was a direct descendant of the Marquis de Sade and refused to accept my pleas of pain. He took hold of my arm and heaved me to my feet, whereupon I promptly passed out. I regained consciousness on a stretcher on my way to a wonderfully warm bed in the military hospital that served all Colchester's barracks. Within a week my back was as good as new and I returned to continue further training.

We were under instruction five and a half days a week, with Saturday afternoons and all of Sunday free, except for church parade in the morning, when I discovered that I was a social outcast. At 09.00 hours on Sunday we donned our best uniforms, fell in outside our quarters and marched to the parade ground. There, a fearsome RSM bawled in stentorian tones, 'All ODs fall out.' In the army, OD stood for 'other denominations', which meant other than Church of England. The C of Es then marched off to church, led by the regimental band, while we odd bods were left to make our way to whatever temple of worship we fancied, or just while away the hours in the town. I decided to seek my God in St Botolph's English Congregational Church.

After the service all the soldiers present were invited to partake of tea and biscuits and meet the local worshippers in the vestry. As a private's weekly pay packet in those days contained the princely sum of 12/6 (62½ pence), free food and drink were very welcome. A private's gross weekly pay was 17/6 (85½ pence) in fact, but 5 shillings (25 pence) was withheld and doled out as a bulk sum when we went on leave. In the vestry we mingled with the local people, who showed us the greatest kindness. A charming, middle-aged couple invited me to share a lunchtime meal with them on the following Sunday and, for the first time since I had left home, I sat down to a sumptuous three-course meal with roast beef and all the trimmings. It was superb. Despite the stringent rationing, the family seemed well supplied with goodies. I discovered later that the father was a grocer, which might explain the comparative abundance! They were kind and generous people and through the six years of war their home was also home to servicemen who, like ships, passed in the night.

The training now was more advanced. We learnt fieldcraft and spent time on the rifle range, learning to shoot and hit stationary and moving targets with Bren guns and rifles. Parade ground drill was a daily event, and we were taught the rudiments of unarmed combat. I was already proficient in Morse code signalling by lamp, flag and key, having learnt my craft in the Home Guard. I was entitled to wear the insignia of a pair of crossed flags on my sleeve, which I did with pride. The flags were noticed and, along with nine others, I was allotted a place on a two-week despatch rider's course. With a 500 cc BSA motorcycle between my legs I was king of the road and countryside. We were taken deep into rural Essex and shown how to handle our bikes over the roughest of rough terrain – along narrow, muddy tracks, through woods, up and down the steep sides of a quarry and through water. I enjoyed every second in the saddle, but not so my room-mate, Percy.

Percy and motorbikes were incompatible. His balance was, at best, precarious, the deep-throated engine's roar intimidated him, and the machine was his master. His participation in the course came to an abrupt end about halfway through. We were gathered on a quarry floor and our instructor demonstrated how to propel the bike up the sloping side and out on to the field at the top. Percy's face was ashen. The technique was simple. Starting at the far end of the quarry, the bike was driven at full throttle across the flat until, on reaching the foot of the incline, the throttle was closed right down. The momentum then carried both bike and rider up to the lip of the quarry without the application of further power. I was first in line. I followed my instructions and sailed up the slope with ease. Percy was next and he was shaking like an aspen leaf. He crossed the quarry bottom like a Hell's Angel, but forgot to shut the throttle as he hit the foot of the slope. He came up over the top, shot into the air and his body parted company with his bike, except for his hands which were cemented to the handlebars in a clamp of terror. The force of gravity brought him back down on to the bike and, stretched at full length from headlamp to the rear end, Percy and bike sped across the field in the direction of a hawthorn hedge. I watched his progress with awe. It ended with the motorcycle passing clean through the hedge, leaving Percy flat on his face at the bottom of it. His helmet and gloves saved him from serious injury, but he flatly refused to even look at, let alone ride, a motorcycle after that.

During my six-week sojourn in Colchester I was always broke by Thursday, and the reason was the quality of the food. The lack of adequate nourishment meant that my mates and I sought succour elsewhere – in the NAAFI canteen. A cup of strong, sweet tea cost a penny (less than a $\frac{1}{2}$ pence), sandwiches and cakes about tuppence (1 pence) each and a good meal could be had for sixpence ($2\frac{1}{2}$ pence). This is where most of our week's pay was spent. We even sacrificed some of our fags to keep body and soul together, until we discovered where we could buy them at rock-bottom prices. A Canadian unit was stationed in an adjoining camp and their troops were always short of cash by Monday, having lavished their pay on Colchester's fair damsels over the weekend. On Monday and Tuesday evenings, British and Canadians met at the camp perimeter and packets of twenty Sweet Carporals were traded for as little as thruppence ($1\frac{1}{2}$ pence) – 'where there's a will, there's a way' and in the army a way was soon found.

After six weeks in Colchester, three months since I had left home and loved ones, I was granted two weeks' leave. For all too brief a period I was reunited with Glen, my family and my friends, and so I made the most of my temporary escape. Glen and I were inseparable. We swam and walked the country lanes as we had always done, yet somehow I felt an alien in a world that I no longer knew. The people and places were unchanged, far removed from the reality of a nation at war, but I had become a very different person in the space of three short months. Of course I was welcomed back like a prodigal son, even Toots the cat was overjoyed. As I walked up the drive to the farmhouse, he saw me, raced forward, sprang and attached himself to my shin in an iron rip. He stayed there, purring loudly, as I walked into the house and it was fully an hour before he let go and climbed on to my shoulder. He disliked Glen intensely. He was not prepared to share my affections with anyone and took to taking sly digs with razor-sharp claws into her nylon-clad legs. The two weeks came to an end all too soon and I had no choice but to return to my other existence, and continue training to become an efficient killer of my fellow men.

Within a week of returning to Goojerat barracks I received my next posting – to the 4th battalion, the Oxfordshire and Buckinghamshire Light Infantry. By this time I was accustomed to the army's ways and no longer felt it strange that I was to serve with a regiment from two English counties that had never seen the imprint of my boot. The 4th was a training battalion, stationed in woodland a mile or so from the golf-coursed, health-resorted, stiff-upper-lipped town of Woodhall Spa in the flatlands of Lincolnshire.

Our platoon of some thirty or so emerging soldiers went on seemingly endless route-marches of twenty to thirty miles a day, and a route-march on the Lincolnshire plain is one of the most soul-destroying experiences I have ever known. The countryside is as flat as a pancake and totally alien to a lad from the bracing air and ever-changing vistas of the Welsh mountains.

In the beginning the route-marches were round trips. We left camp at 09.00 hours and returned some time in the evening. Then came manoeuvres. We deserted our base for several days, marched long distances and made mock attacks on sleepy villages that were held by an imaginary enemy. We were often cold and always hungry, and the kindly villagers slipped us a cup of tea and a slice of cake as we lay on our stomachs by their doorways, waiting for a non-existent enemy to appear. Night exercises were fraught with peril, not from an enemy, but from the many malodorous drainage dykes that criss-crossed the county. In pitch darkness they were invisible and their presence was revealed all too late, when one or more of us fell in. We emerged soaking wet, covered in algal slime and smelling like unripe compost. God, it was cold! But not as cold as the few days and nights that two others and I spent guarding a stretch of silent beach, somewhere near Mablethorpe, against the possibility of invasion. The wind blew unchecked by any barrier (except for us) from the North Sea and the temperature that February hit an all-time low. Our sole defence against the ruthless weather was a draughty Nissen hut, heated by a stove perched in the centre. Even when it was almost white-hot, our backs were ice-cold as we hugged its warmth. No German in his right mind would have given a thought to invading England on those God-forsaken shores. He would have been frozen to the ground before he reached the seaweed line.

Our NCO instructors were battle-hardened survivors of the British Expeditionary Force. They had been plucked from Dunkirk's bloody beaches during the ignominious but mir-aculous retreat and were anxious to impart their knowledge of warfare and the art of survival to us, who had never fired a weapon in anger. They showed us how to survive a sub-zero night in the open with no more cover than what we carried in our packs. Following an evening meal of piping-hot, corned-beef stew, doorsteps of bread and butter and mess tins full of hot, sweet tea, we lay on our backs in a circle of about twelve men, with our feet touching. Clad in greatcoats and lying on our groundsheets, we covered our bodies from toe to chin with our gas capes and donned our woollen Balaclava helmets and gloves. I remember gazing up at a star-studded sky and wondering if I would sleep. I needn't have worried. After a long march, much crossing of fields and ditches at the double, we were all knackered and slept like not-so-innocent babes. We awoke to find the grass around us white with frost. Not only that – we were frozen into a solid, circular block. Each one of us was fused to his neighbours, and the only way to leave our refrigerated repose was to sit up *en masse*. There were no convenient streams, so we washed in the melting hoar frost and even managed a cold shave – a very cold shave, but a good one at that. I suspect that our facial hairs had retreated deep beneath the epidermis to avoid the frost! Breakfast arrived by truck and we marched on full stomachs.

One day I was summoned to the RSMs office and, wondering what sin I had committed, I was marched into the office, ordered to 'stand at ease' and told that as from 24.00 hours, I would be a lance-corporal. I was so stunned and confused that I saluted the RSM, a privilege afforded only to commissioned officers from the rank of Second Lieutenant upwards. The RSM's waxed moustache quivered ever so slightly and the vestige of a smile flickered on his craggy countenance.

In my new-found rank, I was second-in-command of a platoon section and assisted in the training of a series of intakes. So it continued, until my name, along with others, went up on the Company noticeboard. We had been granted fourteen days' embarkation leave prior to posting overseas to a theatre of war. I felt ready for the fray, with one reservation: Glen had left school and joined the Ministry of Defence as a trainee chemical analyst. To further her training, she was despatched to Cambridge to read chemistry relating to explosives. The place was teeming with British and American troops and I felt that she was definitely at risk.

I set off for Cambridge at once. Glen arranged a fortnight's absence from college, and on the morning following my arrival, by the river in the pouring rain, I asked her to marry me. She said, 'yes'. It was the sweetest sounding word. Members of both our families considered that marriage was for mature adults with a future secured by a good job and a guaranteed income. We tackled my family first. Mother was nonplussed, Grandma smiled benignly and Dad, as always, said nothing, adhering to his policy of leaving difficult decisions to my mother. We went through the usual catalogue of objections – we were too young, our future couldn't be more insecure, and so on. I pointed out that if I was old enough to fight for my country, I was surely old enough to get married. From then on, it was no contest and even Dad gave an almost imperceptible sign of approval – he nodded about half an inch. Glen's mother and grandmother (sweet romantics) were in favour. They had known me from short-trouser days and approved of me the man. Her father was a tougher nut to crack. He objected to almost everything in life anyway, and here was an audacious lance-corporal threatening to purloin his daughter, for whom he had affection and high ambitions. We recruited the aid of his mother, the only living being he feared and respected. For over two hours they were closeted in his room, while we all sat in the kitchen to await the verdict that was to determine our future. At last the door opened and Glen's grandmother appeared with a smile creasing her lovely, lived-in face, and we knew that the day was won. Glen's father stayed in his room and never forgave me.

There was no time to lose and the knot was tied the following Sunday. My brand new mother-in-law had somehow prepared a sumptuous wedding breakfast out of the meagre, combined rations of our two families and, together with Glen's bridesmaid and my best man, we tucked in teetotally. The hired car arrived dead on time and my wife and I left to board the bus to Carmarthen.

Neither of us had much money. We were married by special license and it was Glen who paid for it. Hotels were out of the question, so it was decided that we would stay with my aunt and uncle who lived in Nant-y-Caws, a small village three miles from Carmarthen. We arrived in Carmarthen in mist and a fine, relentless drizzle to find that, as it was a Sunday, there were no buses to the village. What of it? We were young, head over heels in love and newly-wed. So we walked the three miles and arrived safely and saturated. Auntie Millie and Uncle John treated us kindly and royally and we enjoyed a memorable honeymoon. It all happened nearly fifty years ago now and the lovely young girl who said, 'yes' and valiantly walked those three miles in high-heeled shoes in the rain is still at my side. I think we would walk it again, if we had to – every step we took then was a preliminary pace, pointing us both to half a century of shared happiness.

My leave ended all too quickly and the day after my return to the unit I was ordered to report to the CO's (Commanding Officer) office. He told me that my overseas posting had been cancelled and I had been recommended for a commission. I was overjoyed. In the same breath the CO told me that I was promoted to a full corporal. The cancellation also meant that Glen and I could be together again, even if only for a short while.

A few weeks later Glen wrote that she was due for a week's leave of absence from the MOD. Could she come and visit me? What a question! That evening I dashed into town and, regardless of expense, booked a double room at the Eagle Lodge Hotel. The middle-aged receptionist was snooty and it showed. I, a mere corporal, was reserving accommodation in Woodhall Spa's most prestigious hostelry, whose guests were either elderly couples of considerable affluence, or army and RAF officers. I'm sure that the old battleaxe believed that I was all set to have an illicit amorous few days with a lady of ill-repute. Her suspicions were confirmed when Glen and I presented ourselves at her desk to sign the register. 'Battleaxe' told me to enter our home address and, without thinking, I turned to Glen and asked, 'Shall I put down yours, or mine?' That did it. Her eyes narrowed and she handed me our room-key with the reluctance of a mother abandoning her only child. We didn't mind. The weekend was ours, but I saw little of Glen during the weekdays as I had to be in camp by 06.00 hours every morning. This meant rising at 05.00 hours to wash, shave and polish before walking to the guard to report in.

On the first morning, my ablutions completed, I kissed my wife goodbye, lit my first Woodbine, descended the stairs and made my way in pitch darkness to the front door. It was locked and there was no key. I stumbled around and then, at the far end of a corridor, I spotted the glow of a cigarette. With a sense of relief I asked, 'Can you please show me the way out of this place?' There was no reply. I advanced and walked smack into a full-length mirror. Thankful that no one had witnessed my embarrassment, I stumbled on until I found a window that opened and made my escape.

Shortly afterwards the battalion moved, lock, stock and barrel, to the market town of Alford at the foot of the Lincolnshire Wolds. I was not sorry to turn my back on Woodhall Spa and its 1940s snobbery. I had been born into and bred in a West Walian, classless society where dustmen rubbed shoulders with doctors, and the only distinction between kindred spirits rested on intellectual prowess. Alford was more like home, populated by warm, friendly people. Proof of their kindness and generosity was shown at Christmas 1943. Glen wrote to say that she had a few days' leave over the holiday period and she would join me if I could find accommodation. With a song in my heart, I began my search for rooms. Everywhere was full. In deep dejection I retraced my steps back to camp. Gloom and despair were my sole companions and, to make matters worse, I was clean out of Woodbines. Then the gods took pity on me. On the outskirts of the town I saw a corner shop, lit up and still open. I bought a packet of ten and, as I had nothing to lose, asked the lady if she knew of anyone who could give my wife and I a room over the Christmas period. She pondered a bit, then suggested that I could try Miss Dogwood at Number — whatever it was. I found the house, rang the bell, pounded the knocker – nothing happened. The hope that had welled, unwelled, but with a last desperate throw I went next door and rang their bell. The woman who answered told me that Miss Dogwood spent every night with her married sister and family, a few streets away. I thanked her and ran to the address I'd been given and there I found my saviour, Miss Dogwood. She was wonderful, superb, magnanimous, generous and every other adjective that may be used to describe an angel come to earth. Glen arrived by train in the late evening, two days before Christmas. Our kind landlady had entrusted me with the key and we entered the empty house to find a fire burning in the grate and a note on the table inviting us to help ourselves to tea and whatever food that took our fancy. Miss Dogwood came home every morning at about 09.00 hours, and if I was on duty at the camp, she took Glen shopping in the town and introduced her to her friends. We had the house to ourselves every night and on Christmas Eve she presented us with a fat, free-range chicken and left to spend Christmas with her family. She trusted us implicitly and I have never met a kinder soul on all this earth.

I remained in Alford with the 4th 'Ox & Bucks' for a further three months, until my posting came through to pre-OCTU (pre-Officer Cadet Training Unit) in Wrotham in Kent. About twenty cadets from various units arrived at the station in the early hours of a Saturday morning. On arrival at the camp we were ordered to leave our kit in the guardroom, have breakfast and report outside A Company Office at 08.30 hours. There, a CSM (Company Sergeant Major) fell us in, in two ranks, and reported us 'all present and correct, sir' to the major on duty. He inspected us briefly and then, to our surprise, gave the order, 'all Welshmen, one step forward, march.' Alone, I stepped forward, to be told by the major, 'You're playing rugby for the unit against Tunbridge Wells. Transport is waiting at the Guard Room. Kit will be provided.' When I asked what I should do with my army kit, he told me to leave it in the Guard Room and collect it on my return. I boarded the truck to join a motley crew of all ranks, ranging from major to private. On the rugby field rank counted for nothing. We played as fifteen fit men, intent on flattening the opposition and scoring tries. We did quite well, the full-time score being nine points to each side. Later, in the large communal bath, we were still equal (more or less!) The visible signs of difference only emerged as we dressed and our respective army ranks reappeared on our sleeves and shoulders. But in that one-off rugby environment we were still on equal terms and I realised that in the army, as in Wales, the game of rugby was a great leveller. Our hosts couldn't have been kinder. After plates of ham and eggs with lashings of bread and butter, we repaired to the bar and drank our fill 'on the house'. We piled back into the truck around midnight and the night air was rent with bawdy arias, as we made the return journey to camp. At one point we were entertained *en route* by a Tank Corps Captain, who recited all the verses of the infamous 'Eskimo Nell' with feeling!

Then an odd thing happened. After a month or so of intensive training, all the occupants of our hut were posted to various OCTUs (Officer Cadet Training Units) all over Britain – all, that is, except for myself and one other soldier. For a whole month we had the hut to ourselves. No one paid us a visit, no one ordered us on parade. We got thoroughly browned off and finally we went to the company office to make enquiries. As far as the clerical staff were concerned, we didn't exist, and I reckon that my companion and I could have spent the rest of the war eating army rations and quaffing pints of good Kentish ale and no one would have been any the wiser. I suspect that our records had been temporarily lost or mislaid. Anyway, someone sorted it out and very shortly I was posted to OCTU in, would you believe, Barmouth on the North Wales coast. I was back in my homeland and Glen was only a shortish bus and train journey away.

I found myself in A Company, stationed in the Cors-y-Gedol hotel in the very centre of the seaside resort. My good fortune continued. I and three other cadets were allocated a large room facing the front, one of only two with large bay windows. It was the fine-weather spring of 1944, and through the open window we observed life in wartime Barmouth. Most of the town's young men were absent in the armed services, but the young girls were still around. The cadets were their prey and their predatory instincts claimed many an unwary man. The few holidaymakers were elderly, mostly escapees from war-torn towns and cities. It was a seaside resort with an air of expectancy, it seemed to be waiting in vain for holidaymakers that would never arrive and for its sons who, hopefully, would return. We were substitute sons and for the sixteen weeks of our 'occupation' we merged into the town's life and ways.

Our training intensified. The key words in all our OCTU training were 'discipline' and 'fitness'. Discipline was in the very capable hands of a part-time tyrant. He stood 6 feet 6 inches in his socks. His back was as straight and true as a ramrod, and the hairs of his waxed moustache were equally distributed and angled on each side of his upper lip. He was a Coldstream Guardsman and a fearsome figure of a man. The parade ground was a concreted, peacetime playground, conspicuously situated on the very centre of the promenade. It was here that for an hour every day he put us through our paces. We marched up and down, right- and left-wheeled, halted, ordered arms, sloped arms, presented arms and would have been ordered to inwardly digest arms if our RSM had thought the feat remotely possible! There were times when I admit we were a trifle sluggish. A favourite ploy was to send our company on a five-mile run in denim uniforms and carrying our Lee Enfield rifles. On our return we were allowed ten minutes to change from denim to serge uniforms and present ourselves on the square for an hour's arms drill, and all this on a warm summer's morning very often. It is not surprising that we were not at our best and, for the RSM, nothing but the best was good enough. As we marched around the square, he plied us with insults until he brought us to a halt and, in a voice that could be heard in Ireland, we were informed, 'You are worse than the washerwomen of Barmouth'. This was a downright lie because, as far as we knew, he had never tried to drill a company of local laundresses! When, at times, we still failed to reach the required standard, he issued the dreaded order: 'At the double, quick march, left wheel' and we were over the prom and double-marching in loose sand. Anyone that collapsed, or even lagged a little, was accused of being 'You idle man' and given extra duties.

He didn't have it all his own way though. There was the memorable occasion when, having put us through his whole range of tortures, he brought us back to the square, stood us at ease and proceeded to tell us in livid language that we were the lowest form of human life and weren't fit to wear the King's uniform. Without warning and still in full spate he was interrupted by a little elderly lady, bearing a rolled-up umbrella. She approached our RSM with a purposeful stride, shouted at him that he was treating us worse than animals and belted him over the head with her umbrella. He straightened his cap, drew himself to his full height and in honeyed tones said, 'Madam, it is my job to train and discipline these men to go to war, take charge of troops and return safely when it is all over. May I carry on?' From that moment, he had our unqualified admiration and respect and we would have followed him into the jaws of hell. Of such stuff are great leaders made.

During the final weeks at OCTU most of our training was tactical. We went on night marches and manoeuvres that entailed finding our way back to base by the stars and a compass. Our most valuable asset on these outings was Phil. She was a lady who ran a kind of super-tuckshop in a small, wooden hut by the level crossing in the town centre. Her sandwiches were as thick as patio slabs and filled with delicious concoctions. We kept her informed of our night manoeuvres and Phil, bless her strong tea, stayed open to satisfy our hunger when we returned in the early hours. She was a morale booster beyond compare. An Army marches on its stomach, so it is said and, thanks to Phil, our steps never faltered.

It was on a protracted exercise that I came across a family who were the epitome of contentment. Our company left base for a week-long series of marches and mock battles in the mountainous reaches of, what was then, Merionethshire. At the end of each day we made camp wherever we happened to be and, as the days and nights were fair, we bivouaced under cloudless skies. We lived on iron rations consisting mainly of sandwiches, biscuits, cheese, corned-beef and soup made from a powdered concentrate and boiling water. Our first priority was a 'brew up', as there is nothing better to restore flagging bodies and spirits than a good 'cuppa'. While the tea was brewing, I took a stroll across some open ground to a high, dry-stone wall, and some distance away I spotted a small, stone-built cottage nestling in the crook of the mountain. I made my way towards it and, as I drew near, I saw that there were three people seated side by side on a wooden bench by the front door. The white-bearded old man puffed contentedly on a churchwarden pipe, the old lady was shelling peas and the younger woman just sat, gazing dreamily into the golden setting sun. A Welsh sheepdog lay at her feet and a clutch of hens scratched and foraged around them. There was a feeling of perfect peace. The dog regarded me with deep suspicion, as indeed did the three rustics on the bench.

Within a few yards of them, I said, *'Noswaith dda'* (good evening). The effect was electric. All three froze momentarily, then their weathered faces were wreathed in smiles as they returned my greeting. I spoke their language and they accepted me into their solitary circle, set in a world beyond our ken. The nearest village was several miles away and the young woman, the daughter, made the round trip once a month on foot, to exchange eggs and plucked chickens for basic provisions. It was their only contact with the outside world. I sat with them in the balmy evening air while the old man plied me with questions. He knew there was a war on, but who with? They listened intently while I tried to acquaint them with the current events in a turbulent world that stood in stark contrast to their idyllic existence. In the twilight I bade them farewell and went with a gift of a dozen fresh eggs and the promise that I would call again. I kept my promise and on duty-free Saturdays I borrowed one of the company's 'bone-shakers' (bikes) and made my way to that lonely, lovely cottage on the hill and the three innocents who dwelt there. I bought a dozen eggs for a shilling (5 pence) on each visit and became exceedingly popular with my room-mates on my return.

Our week-long exercise ended with a concerted assault down the mountainside across half a mile of open ground and on to a beach where an imaginary invasion was in progress. It was helter-skelter all the way and, by the time we hit the sand on that hot summer's day, perspiration was pouring down our grime-encrusted bodies. In short, we stank of sweat and accumulated dirt. The sea was blue, calm and tempting and I requested 'permission to swim, sir'. Within seconds a hundred and twenty stark naked men tore down the beach and hurled themselves into the ocean. Never before, or since, has so much male flesh been exposed and disported on any North Walian beach. What a sight it was! It was just as well that the dunes and the beach were deserted. Now, fifty years later, the mock invasion is a reality. The once secluded foreshore and dunes are pockmarked with caravans and, except for the scrounging seagulls, most of the wildlife has departed to more peaceful places.

Barmouth is a small resort, wedged between the waters of Cardigan Bay and the cliffs that rise steeply and dominate the town. I liked nothing better than to climb the cliff paths on a summer's evening and watch the sun sink over the horizon in a red ball of fire. It was so peaceful up there among the rocks and lichens, with only the birds for company. I wished that Glen could share the countryside's tranquil solitude with me and, on one wonderful long weekend, she came and joined me in a boarding house in the town. Fortune smiled on us. Saturday and Sunday were gloriously sunny and we took to the mountains with a packed lunch and a flask of tea. We discovered private places where two people in love could find utter fulfilment in each other's company. The pains of parting and the threats of war were forgotten in a fleeting present, so joyous that we were oblivious of the uncertainty of the future – and it came to pass that Glen was with child! We were both overjoyed.

The climax of the four months at OCTU was the passing

out parade and I was one of the many cadets that completed the metamorphosis from corporal to one-pip Second Lieutenant. The fire-breathing RSM became human and, shaking each one of us by the hand, he wished us good luck and a happy return. And so we went our various ways – I to the 9th Royal Welch Fusiliers training battalion in Crickhowell, for training as a platoon commander and to await an overseas posting. I took my platoon up and down the Brecon Beacons, across rivers and anywhere else where life was at its most uncomfortable. The first clue to my future destination came when I was sent on a short course to Matlock, to be instructed in jungle warfare, in theory if not in practice, seeing that there are no jungles in Derbyshire! Oddly enough, we were also taught to count from one to ten in Japanese. I can't imagine that attacking a Jap stronghold yelling, 'ichi, ni, san, yon, go, roku' (or something like that) would have frightened the life out of the enemy – surprised them, yes.

On my return from Matlock, and on orders from above, I took my platoon to Llangattock, near Llandovery, for yet more training and received news that the arrival of Clay-Jones Junior was imminent. I immediately applied for a few days' compassionate leave, which was granted by an equally compassionate CO. On the third of February 1945 our daughter was born and to celebrate the momentous event, Valmai, my sister-in-law, and I went for a swim. It was a glorious, sun-kissed day and it seemed right somehow, in a world that was crazy anyhow. I had three days with my wife and daughter before returning to my unit, and then within a few days I was on a train to Liverpool, to board the SS *Windsor Castle, en route* to Bombay. As the ship edged away from the dockside, I leant on the rails, gazed at the Liver Birds with a heavy heart, and couldn't help wondering whether I would see dear old Blighty and the people that made my life worth living again. I was not alone. Hundreds of khaki-clad men lined the rails, their eyes filled with the pain of parting. Those of us who believed in a

God, prayed for deliverance, the others prayed just as hard to no one in particular. The one thing we had in common was that we were all 'licenced to kill' and on our way.

Foreign Fields

℘

O N board ship I found myself in a cabin with another officer of equal rank. Space, though limited, was adequate and on the toss of a coin I was fortunate in laying claim to the bottom bunk of a double-decker. There were sixteen SWBs (South Wales Borderers) other ranks in my charge billeted in rather cramped but comfortable quarters in the bowels of the ship. Having inspected their quarters, I knew that my merry men would become bored and start searching for trouble unless provided with something to relieve the monotony. It is said that two or more Welshmen marooned on a desert island would (a) appoint a committee, (b) build a chapel, or (c) form a choir. The first two options were non-starters, but the third had distinct possibilities. On the second night out of port I assembled my sixteen ORs (other ranks) up on deck, found a quiet corner and, with a swagger stick in hand, led them in a verse of 'Ar hyd y nos' ('All through the night'), followed by the hymn beloved of all Taffs, and rugby players in particular, 'Cwm Rhondda' or 'Guide me, O thou great Jehovah'. By the time we got to 'feed me till I want no more' our numbers had more than doubled. There were tenors and baritones and a choir worthy of the Albert Hall (almost)! Among the volunteer choristers was Lieutenant Joe Evans, and together we knocked our impromptu singers into shape. Also on board was an ENSA (Entertainments National Services Association) concert party bound for Port Said, where they were to disembark and organise shows for the 8th Army. We joined forces and put on a show most nights. The choir's

87

pièce de résistance was a rendering of 'The Holy City' with myself as soloist. Our efforts were always very well received, because we had a captive audience!

The Bay of Biscay was in a filthy mood. Mountainous seas met us, the huge ship pitched and rolled, and most of the ship's pressganged passengers lay groaning and grey in their bunks. Having been fortunate enough to be born with a pair of sea-legs, I found myself at breakfast, the sole occupant of our circular eight-seater table. The food on board was superb, up to peacetime standards, and I took advantage. On that morning I chose kippers, a delicacy I had not seen for months in ration-bound Britain. A plate the size of hub-caps duly arrived and on it lay two huge, fat and fleshy kippered herrings. They were delicious and the steward, who had observed my voracious destruction of the fish, asked, 'Would you like another helping, sir?' Having disposed of eight cooked-to-a-turn kippers, I left, replete. The steward became a firm friend. He admired my disregard of the ship's erratic progress and admired even more my capacity for good food.

Also on board, bound for the 8th Army, was a Shakespearian company led by the incomparable Donald Wolfit. After we passed Gibraltar and entered the placid waters of the Mediterranean, the theatre company treated us to performances of *Macbeth* and *The Merchant of Venice*. Such was their mastery of their craft that they held a large audience of squaddies enthralled from start to finish. It was all the more remarkable, because they performed both plays on a hatch cover on the open deck, with their audience squatting on the bare boards around them. It was theatre in the round and in the raw. My squaddies loved it and wrote letters home in lavish praise, although one read: 'Dear Mum and Dad, today we saw *The Merchant of Venus*' – Well, he wasn't far wrong, was he? I was aware of the *faux pas* because I had the task of censoring all letters and blue-pencilling anything that could be of value to the enemy.

One morning in the Med remains forever in my memory. I am, by nature, an early riser and I was usually washed, shaved and up on deck as dawn turned to day. The ship was at anchor, not a ripple troubled the glassy, calm waters and through the rising vapours a small township shimmered in the early light. I was alone. Not a sound reached my ears and for a few moments the war belonged to another world. Here was peace, perfect peace, with no human sight or sound to sully the idyllic scene.

In Bombay we disembarked and boarded a waiting troop train bound for the infamous transit camp, known to countless British soldiers as 'Doolaly', but more properly spelt 'Deolali'. The camp was a long-established conglomeration of buildings stuck in the middle of nowhere. The surrounding countryside was depressingly flat. Nothing seemed to grow and temperatures soared to over 100°F. Many of the permanent staff had been known to lose their mental balance, hence the term, 'Doolaly Tap'. To this day, anyone in the army showing signs of eccentricity is considered to have 'a touch of the Doolaly's,' originally contracted by long service east of Suez. My respite in that place was brief, but long enough to experience my first Indian haircut. A towering Sikh arrived outside my door, complete with wooden hard-backed chair, towel, scissors and comb. He set up shop on the parched earth, sat me down, cut my locks and then proceeded to apply a vigorous scalp massage. It entailed an attempted penetration of my cranium with digits of steel, alternating with a pounding of the whole head. He spoke good English, so I enquired the reason for the apparent assault on my person. His reply may be of value to all sparsely covered men of all ages – 'Keep blood coming to head, *sahib*, no go bald.' It makes sense and I still have a good head of hair.

On arrival at Deolali my draft of sixteen ORs was handed over to a platoon sergeant and within a couple of weeks I was on my way again by train, on a remarkable journey across the Indian continent to Bangalore in the State of Madras. I'm not quite sure whether the journey took twelve or fourteen days, but it was sheer purgatory.

I was now a two-pip lieutenant, as were two travelling

companions who, like myself, were both named Jones – Bryn and L. A. G. Jones who, inevitably, was christened 'Lag'; we never discovered his Christian names. The three of us occupied a compartment peculiar to Indian trains. It comprised a bathroom, complete with sink and rusty bath, and quite a spacious living-room equipped with three bunks – a single and a double-decker. Above our abode, and occupying its entire length, was a full tank of water for our ablutions. We tossed a coin for bunks and I lost. My companions took the two ground-floor bunks, leaving me with the top bunk immediately beneath the water tank. The Indian summer was at its peak and within hours of setting off the water temperature in the uninsulated tank heated to near boiling point under the relentless sun. During the day we passed the dreary hours playing cards, gazing at the Indian countryside and steeling ourselves to tackle our next meal.

We had a stock of American K rations in small, individual cardboard boxes, labelled respectively with the initials B for breakfast, L for lunch and D for dinner. For what it is worth, the contents were almost identical, and they contained a quantity of rock-hard biscuits, so hard that by the journey's end our mouths had lost several layers of skin. As one of us remarked, 'I know that these are iron rations, but they might have provided us with a file!' These tinned, concentrated, dehydrated consumables were our daily fare, which we supplemented by purchasing fresh oranges and bananas from the many vendors that haunt every station in India. We stored these in the bath, which proved incapable of performing the function for which it had been fashioned. The steam train thundered across the Continent day and night, pausing only briefly at some stations and for longer periods at 11.00 hours and again at about 19.00 hours when the train driver and his mate felt the pangs of hunger. Then the train came to a halt anywhere. The two men dismounted, made a fire of red-hot coals from the boiler and proceded to brew a can of tea and cook a curry and a few *chapatis* (Indian bread). The appetising, tantalising aroma drifted along the carriages and we eyed our own meagre rations with increasingly jaundiced eyes. For the most part, our Trans-Continental journey was boringly monotonous, but from time to time the flora and fauna of this great land was new and fascinating. Mango and palm trees sped past, herds of water buffalo wallowed in mud, flamingos rose in a flutter of panic as we approached, skinny dogs barked, children waved and we observed the natives going about their leisurely lives. The war still seemed remote and unreal. I slept little and fitfully, spending most nights sitting by the open carriage door, lulled by the cool night air into a restful stupor.

In Bangalore we were greeted by the station master and conducted to a dining-room, where we sat down to the first cooked meal we had seen for many a day. From Bangalore we travelled to a Jungle Warfare Training Camp in the Nilgiri Hills in the State of Mysore. It was a designated Nature Reserve, which meant that the resident animals accepted our intrusion into their territory with a benign indifference. Respecting the Maharajah's wishes, firearms were not used, and we concentrated solely on acclimatising ourselves to the claustrophobia of the jungle and on fieldcraft and junglecraft. The Far Eastern jungle is all-embracing, but in the Nilgiri Hills it was not unduly oppressive. At the end of the war Spencer Chapman wrote a book entitled *The Jungle Is Neutral*, which illustrated how friend and foe are equal within the jungle's bounds. However, the jungle affects men differently. There were hidden dangers, and in Nilgiri we learnt to avoid fruits that looked temptingly tasty, but were deadly poisonous. We learnt how to identify poisonous snakes, scorpions and other animals that were far from human-friendly, and it was drummed into us that the malaria-carrying mosquito was the British soldier's worst enemy.

Practical training involved the art of silent advance, the methods of patrolling in small groups by day and by night and how to cross deep rivers in the absence of a boat, but keeping all our equipment dry. This last manoeuvre was accomplished with the aid of bamboo – the jungle fighter's best friend. There cannot be a more utilitarian plant in the whole world. Its tall, straight stems are felled easily and quickly with a *machete*, or a *kukhri*, which is a Gurkha knife, equally effective at chopping down trees or beheading animals and enemies. A foot long, the curved blade of tempered steel is sharp enough to split hairs and skulls, and at the base of the blade, by the handle, there is a convenient double notch that prevents blood from staining and desecrating the hand of the wielder. Many's the time we saw a Gurkha decapitate a goat with one clean whoosh of the blade, prior to skinning the animal and preparing a scrumptious curry. With a *kukhri* in hand, we learnt to do all kinds of things with bamboo. We made tables, beds, knives and forks with it and, time permitting, we could have constructed a hut in less than a day. To cross rivers, lengths of female bamboo were lashed together. We loaded our kit on to them and swam, pushing the raft across. The trunks of male bamboo are solid, but the females are hollow. Not only are they light and buoyant, but they usually also contain water in internal compartments – a boon when it is a scarce commodity. The water is clean and crystal clear and tastes of bamboo, but for a parched foot soldier it was often the elixir of the gods. We also ate bamboo. The young shoots of the new growths are pale, tender and, we were assured, nutritious, but as they have the flavour of feeble camphor, they found favour with no one.

Our stay in the Nilgiri camp was brief, but invaluable, and there were leisure periods that we used according to our individual whims. Most of us walked the half-mile path down to a river and either swam, or played a primitive version of water polo, watched by several species of monkeys who, judging by their noise and antics, found the sight of naked white men hilarious.

Before breakfast I walked the jungle path to the river pool alone, except for the local fauna. Monkeys with a frill of fine grey hair encircling their faces grinned and cackled, a six-foot-long yellow snake once crossed my path and slithered into the undergrowth, even more scared than I was, and one magical morning a young slender deer preceded me down to the water, oblivious of my presence, and drank deeply. I also walked along along some of the paths that led into deeper jungle. Perhaps I was foolish, but it was worth it. I watched a chameleon move and change its camouflage. I saw magnificent, multi-coloured butterflies and other insects and innumerable exotic plants and flowers. How I regret that I didn't have a camera and that my biological knowledge was so basic and confined to my homeland. On one of my jaunts I even saw a tiger. It was getting dark as I approached camp one night along a narrow trail, when I sensed I was being followed. I spun round on my heel and there, about a hundred yards away, stood this beast. As I turned, he turned and in a second vanished into the undergrowth. In another second I was back in camp, having broken all sprint records.

In those green-clad hills the war was still impersonal, but not for very much longer. Bryn, Lag and I got our final posting. We were to join the 2nd battalion the Welch Regiment in 62 Brigade 19th Indian (Dagger) Division – so called because its insignia was a golden dagger on a red background. Mandalay had fallen and the Division was driving the Japs back down towards Rangoon on the southern tip of Burma. The three of us left Nilgiri, and journeyed up the Bramaputra River to Chittagong, yet another transit camp, to await transportation into Burma. Our conveyance turned out to be an American Dakota, piloted by a gum-chewing, taciturn Texan. All he said was, 'git in,' so we did. The body of the plane was completely empty, so we sat on our bedrolls and leant against the fuselage. Our flight over the Chindit mountain range was comparable to a ride on Blackpool's Big Dipper. As we crossed the peaks and deep valleys, the plane either dropped like a stone or rocketed upwards as it hit the thermals and, to cap it all, we flew through an electrical storm. The plane's sides went in and out like a wheezy accordion and it seemed to me that it was only a matter of time before all four of us would be joining the heavenly chorus. The pilot remained taciturn and unconcerned throughout, calmly chewing gum and drawing deeply on a fat cigar.

We made Meiktila and landed without further incident on the makeshift runway to the sound of gunfire. I, 324279 Lieutenant Clay-Jones, was at war. A 15 cwt truck took us along a shell-holed road to Battalion HQ where we reported to our Commanding Officer, Lt Colonel 'Bun' Cowey. Pre-war he had played rugby for Wales. I knew we were in good hands.

19th Indian Division comprised three brigades under the command of a short, stocky son of a South Wales clergyman – Major General T. Wynford Rees, known to his British troops at 'Pete' for some reason. To his Indian troops he was General *Sahib Bahadur* or the 'lion-hearted'. He neither smoked nor drank alcoholic liquor. He was a brilliant tactician who sensed the enemy's next move before he made it, and his courage was legendary. To the consternation of his staff, he would pop up in the heat of battle to boost morale, and we all loved the little firebrand of a man. In addition to the 2nd Welch, 62 Brigade had two other battalions – the 3rd/6th Rajputana Rifles and 4th/6th Gurkhas, together with a Sikh Armoured Car Unit and the usual medical and other back-up troops.

62 Brigade was as fine a body of fighting men as ever laid into an enemy and the 2nd Welch had acquitted themselves with honour, as the Japs were driven back from the very frontiers of India. In orderly retreat, the Japs were still fighting with the fanaticism peculiar to a nation who believed that their ruler was God and therefore defeat was impossible, let alone unthinkable. 19 Division pushed southwards from Meiktila, until the town of Toungoo was taken. The 2nd Welch established its HQ in the town at the foot of the Mawchi Road, up which the enemy were retreating in strength and leap-frogging eastwards through an endless series of fiercely resisting strongholds. We were in hot pursuit and lost a number of men to sniper fire; we were constantly aware of this invisible threat. Shelling was not a worry, and we grew accustomed to the sound of shells ripping through the trees above our heads and exploding harmlessly before they came to earth. We had advanced some way up the Mawchi Road when the monsoon broke – and when I say broke, I mean broke. We were in one

of the worst malarial regions in the Far East and with the monsoon the mosquito population multiplied. Every man was compelled by Army Regulations to swallow one Mepacrin tablet daily, to ward off the dreaded disease that, at best, lays men low and, at worst, is a killer. It was every officer's duty to see that each man complied with the order.

In fact, during the monsoon, disease reduced our numbers far more than the Japanese enemy. Men were brought to a halt by attacks of jaundice, dysentery and occasionally by unidentified sicknesses peculiar to the jungle. Jungle sores were vile and nasty. They appeared inexplicably and initially as little more than a pimple. An affected area turned rapidly into an open, pus-filled sore which was not painful in itself, but extremely tender to the touch. Out on patrol under the dripping jungle canopy we were also plagued by leeches – horrible, slimy, slug-like creatures that sank their fangs into the skin and drank their fill of blood. When they were satiated and could drink no more, they dropped off, leaving a bleeding wound that turned septic unless treated. Patrolling in single file, every man kept a wary eye on the fellow in front and when a leech appeared on his person, a halt was called, a match lit and applied to the disgusting predator. A lighted match, or a pinch of salt on their tails was the only way to be rid of the blood-suckers. Once, a leech managed somehow to enter my boot, presumably through one of the bootlace eyelets. The first I knew of its presence was when my right foot began to squelch as I walked. I removed the boot to find both sock and foot red with blood and a squashed leech at my ankle. These were the atrocious conditions under which friend and foe alike fought each other, the elements and pestilence.

Somehow we managed to maintain our men's morale and our own. We were well aware that we were the 'forgotten army' and knew that the war on the European front commanded the almost exclusive attention of the British media and the people. On a visit to his front-line troops, the 14th Army Commander, General 'Bill' Slim, uttered the immortal words as he addressed a gathering of war-weary men: 'You are not forgotten. Nobody knows you bloody exist.' Superb commander and psychologist that he was, he was cheered to the echo.

The monsoon continued with relentless intensity, with rain coming down in unbroken sheets of warm water. At intervals the weather cleared, and we were steam-dried in the oppressive, clammy, tropical humidity. The Mawchi Road wound its way steeply upwards into the mountains, making frontal attacks suicidal. The only alternative was to approach the enemy position from its flanks, which entailed several days of plodding along jungle tracks until a favourable attacking position was reached. One such operation proved extremely arduous. On the second or third day we left the track and continued our advance through horrendously difficult terrain. I was a platoon commander and I should have had thirty men under my command. In reality, disease and enemy action had reduced our numbers to the point where I was the only platoon commander under the irrepressible, 'immortal' Major Carter. He sported a monocle and a malacca cane and where the rest of us scuttled across paths and open ground, 'old Carter' strolled nonchalantly, as though it was a village lane on a quiet Sunday morning. His total disregard for the safety of his own skin was, I'm sure, deliberate, and his way of quelling the fear of us lesser mortals.

Both his and our strength and stamina were tested to the limit on this particular flanking movement. The monsoon was still at its height and, although we were in deep jungle, there was little undergrowth except for fairly dense grassy vegetation. The rain had beaten it flat, making an uphill advance difficult. We were several miles from base and, in the absence of a supply team, we carried a considerable weight of ammunition, including 3-inch mortar shells and, theoretically, enough rations to last until we had completed our operation and regained the Mawchi Road. For every three steps we took up the slippery slopes, we slid two back and by the end of the day we were exhausted. Officers were expected to set a good example and so, having reached the summit, Major Carter and

I went back down more than once to help in heaving the ammunition boxes etc to the top. It was at the end of one such strength-sapping day that I collapsed and began shivering uncontrollably. My legs gave way and I felt like death warmed up. My platoon sergeant, the indefatigable, tower-of-strength, second-in-command Sergeant Crome, recognised that I was in the throes of heat exhaustion, brought on by dehydration allied to a low blood-salt level. I was made to swallow three salt tablets swilled down with a pint of precious water, sacrificed from several water-bottles. Within minutes I was back on my feet and feeling fit enough to go ten rounds with any heavy-weight world champion.

I will never forget the tragic end of one of my men on this operation. We were almost within reach of our objective and, having scaled yet another saturated peak, we made camp, dug our foxholes, brewed up, saw to our wounded and gave each man his rum ration, which was issued only when it was deemed that the human body was nearing the limit of endurance. Our cook had knocked up a corned-beef stew and as I sat and savoured it, one of my men came up and said simply, 'I think Private Davies is in a bad way, sir.' I couldn't believe it. I had seen him a half-hour or so previously when I made my rounds, and he had seemed well enough then. Davies' foxhole was on the perimeter of our position and when I reached him it was obvious that something was seriously wrong. He hadn't touched his food and was lying prone alongside his foxhole. He was, by army standards, elderly. Most of us were in our early twenties, but Davies was in his mid-thirties and I naturally thought that he was merely exhausted. I was assured that he had drunk plenty of water with salt tablets, but when I tried to induce him to eat his meal, he replied that he wasn't hungry and that he had lost all feeling in his feet. I stayed with him as the numbness crept from his feet up his legs and up his torso, until it reached his heart and he died. He didn't panic. He just kept telling me how the creeping paralysis was progressing until finally he closed his eyes and departed this life. We wrapped him in a blanket, lowered him into his foxhole and I prayed for his safe deliverance to a better place, before we covered him and erected a simple bamboo cross bearing his name, rank, and number.

We were still heavily laden with the weapons of war, but our provisions were exhausted. A signal was sent to HQ, and the order came back to clear a patch of jungle for a supply airdrop. It was a new exciting experience for most of us. The clearing was marked with strips of white cloth, then we heard the drone of an aircraft, and a Dakota hove into sight. A cheer went up and we promptly ran for our lives. All but two of the heavy bales floated gently down on their parachutes; the others came plummeting earthwards at the end of unopened chutes with a force that would have flattened anyone in their path. We tore the bales open and feasted on tins of jam, cheese, evaporated milk, 'herrings-in', meat, fruit and the inescapable 'hard-tack' biscuits.

The day I joined the 2nd Welch I had asked for a volunteer to act as my batman. An immediate response came from Private Gordon Hynes, who soon proved to be more of a companion than a servant. Behind the lines he kept my clothing and equipment in sparkling condition and at the front he saw to it that I never went short of anything that was going. He could produce a fag when I was desperate, and cups of tea appeared as if by magic in the most unlikely situations. In his backpack he carried a crib-board and a pack of cards and in the lull between battles we played with matches worth millions of pounds. He too survived, went home, got married and now lives happily with his wife in Swansea. I know all this because we met again in unexpected circumstances many, many years later, but more of that in due course.

Toungoo in the monsoon was under two feet of water. It was an annual event, which is why houses on the Burmese plain are built on stilts, with several feet of clearance between the ground and the living quarters. During the monsoon an odd thing happened. Before the rains came, the earth was parched and bone-dry, but within hours, as the water rose, the whole area teemed with fish that came, apparently, from nowhere. I saw black, slimy and repulsively tentacled catfish, but there were many others that resembled our native species and looked good enough to eat. I failed to catch a single one, but the locals captured them in quantity, ate some and dried the surplus. At this time, Burmese towns and villages stank like stale-fish shops. A strong stench of fish meal pervaded the air, as the fish dried in the sun on bamboo mats. When they were as desiccated as prunes, they were powdered, stored and used to flavour meals of all kinds.

The Battalion, including D Company, made several more successful sorties up the Mawchi Road and each one took its toll on our men. Our general health was at a low ebb and our CO decided that a part of the battalion, including D Company, should head for the cleaner, drier, cooler air of the high mountains above the tree-line. My platoon was the first to leave, bound for the small village of Thandaung at an altitude of 4,600 feet.

The prospect of leaving the heat of the Burma plain in exchange for the crisp and cooler air of the wood-clad mountains appealed to us all. On a morning in July, I 'fell in' some thirty D Company personnel, inspected them and gave the order to embus. Our transport was an open 5-ton truck captured from the Japs and, accompanied by two jeeps, we headed for the hills and Thandaung. Our small convoy climbed the steep, tortuous road with the men in high spirits, in anticipation of a welcome respite from war and worry. On arrival we established our HQ in a large disused tea factory on the fringes of what had been an extensive and prosperous pre-war tea plantation. We posted the regulation sentries and settled down to enjoy a short period of untroubled living, or so I believed. I was wrong, terribly wrong.

Knowing that a further detachment of men was scheduled to join us on the morrow, I received orders to take out a motorised patrol at 09.00 hours and scour the plantation for possible signs of the enemy. At the appointed hour I set off with eight fully-armed men in two jeeps, escorted by a Sikh-manned armoured car that had joined us the previous evening.

CLAY

We had gone some way along our patrol route when one keen-eyed member of our patrol spotted a lone British soldier walking along the road several miles below us. He shouldn't have been there and I immediately felt a cold chill of apprehension. We about-turned our small column and headed downhill at full speed. The man was indeed one of ours. His back was pock-marked with grenade splinters and in shell-shocked calm he told his terrible, tragic tale. We left him to walk the short distance to our newly established camp and made our way down the mountain to the scene of carnage he had described.

Even now my blood runs cold as the memory of what met our eyes comes reluctantly to mind. The transport we had used the previous day had returned to Toungoo and on this fateful morning had reloaded with a further consignment of about thirty of our men. Unknown to us, our journey the previous day had been observed by a large party of Japs heading for the comparative safety of Indo-China. Surmising, correctly, that our convoy was a daily event they had lain in wait, and as the three vehicles rounded the corner they opened up with rifles, machine-guns and grenades. It was a massacre. The Sikh truck-driver and his two companions in the cab had been killed instantly. The floor of the open lorry was strewn with bodies and a pile of our dead lay under the chassis, where they had fruitlessly sought safety. In that lovely place lay too many lifeless men who had died for no other reason than that they were in the wrong place at the wrong time. I wept with rage; later, much later, I wept with sorrow. For the first time in my life I was all too aware of the futility of war, of its cruelty and of man's inhumanity to man. We found four men, wounded but alive, and took them back with us to base. We buried our dead, thanked God for the gift of life and went about our business, seemingly as before. I now know that on that July day I really came of age. My life had been spared and thenceforth I have valued each day's dawn, faced trials and tribulations without a qualm, and have been content with my lot – but I still remember.

The daily perimeter patrols continued without further incident and we also undertook patrols into areas where the presence of Japanese had been reported. The reports arrived at HQ in the guise of a small, wizened old Burmese fellow who was tattooed from head to foot and spoke English. We received him in our office and, with words and gestures, the dye-stained midget imparted his information as to the location of a detachment of enemy troops in the locality. His reward was a tin mug, full to the brim with Trinconopoli XXX Rum, an alcoholic beverage powerful enough to strip paint off walls! Our rum ration was a third of a mugful, diluted with water. In fact, one of our men once drank half that quantity of the undiluted firewater and passed out for several hours. Our wizened informant drank the whole mugful in one gargantuan swallow, saluted and walked away, grinning broadly. I am now convinced that the tidings he brought were fictitious, merely figments of his imagination brought on by an unquenchable thirst for strong drink.

Within a couple of weeks we were back in Toungoo, whilst another company took to the mountain air of Thandaung, and once again we went 'up the Mawchi Road'. The enemy had dug in just beyond a bridge that spanned a normally quiet stream, now a raging, wide torrent with the incessant monsoon rains. D Company set up a position straddling the road on our side of the bridge, at a vantage point overlooking the enemy position. We made plans and preparations to attack, but when morning came our patrol discovered that the Japs had abandoned their position and withdrawn. Their patrols had undoubtedly reported that they were heavily outnumbered and their commander had come to the conclusion that discretion was the better part of valour.

Then came more good news. I had taken a patrol of four or five men to ascertain the lie of the land and, on our return, found a welcome cup of 'char' waiting for us. I took mine to my foxhole and as I sat there, sipping the camellian nectar, Sergeant Crome walked over. He was a man of very few words and, sitting himself by my side, he remarked casually, 'The

war's over, sir. The Yanks have dropped a big bomb on Japan.'
I couldn't believe my ears. After six long years of death and
deprivation, was it really true that there was peace in the
world, that we would fight no more, that we could go home
to our loved ones, that we could take up where we had left
off? Was it really true? In that far-off land, in a silent, foreign
jungle where even the animals had fled in the face of gunfire –
I needed a lot of convincing. But it was true. A ruthless enemy
who chose death, rather than surrender, and who neither gave,
nor expected quarter, had waved the white flag. Victory had
cost dear. From November 1944 to VJ day in August 1945, the
2nd Battalion, the Welch Regiment had lost seventeen officers
and three hundred and eight men. They paid the high price of
peace.

Everyone who fought as a PBI (poor bloody infantryman)
in the Burma campaign, did so under the most appalling cli-
matic and topographical conditions of any theatre of war.
Somehow, the true grit of the British Tommy overcame all
adversity and somehow, he remained undaunted, cheerful and
firm in his resolution that victory would be ours. His oft-
quoted motto: *nil carborundum illegitimi* (don't let the bastards
grind you down) raised his spirits in the darkest hours. In
Burma the terrain dictated that the infantryman, be he Indian,
Gurkha, British or whatever nationality, bore the brunt of battle
and Nature's hostility. The British who served in Burma
deserve the Nation's respect, admiration and gratitude and
I'm proud that I can say, 'I was there.'

The Peace

❧

THERE was still much to be done before we could all make tracks for home. Those who had served longest in India and Burma were repatriated almost immediately, leaving behind a depleted army of occupation. The fighting done, we deserted the jungle and its natural hazards and life became more pleasant day by day. In some ways, our lot improved shortly after the war in Europe ended. Truckloads of welfare parcels began to arrive for the very first time, their contents donated by the public and organised for despatch by the tireless ladies of the Women's Institute, the Women's Voluntary Service, the Red Cross and other groups. Presumably because these ladies had no idea what life was like in Burma, or even where it was, the parcels contained, among other things, hand-knitted woollen gloves, mitts, scarves and Balaclava helmets. But very welcome were the tins of British cigarettes and pipe tobacco, especially the cigarettes. For most of the time we had smoked nothing but Indian-made Woodbines, and one needed to be deft and a dedicated smoker to puff on them. The packet was a replica of the British version, except that it was coloured brown and not green. As for the tobacco, it was darker in colour and in the dry pre-monsoon heat it fell out of its paper tube, unless one removed the cigarette horizontally. When lit, it had the aroma and flavour of an autumn bonfire, but it was better than nothing. Most of us were fag fanatics, so the tinned pipe tobacco was given to the local Burmese, along with the woollen garments. Most of them chewed the tobacco, but goodness knows what they did with the woollies. Possessed of the Cardi's inborn thrift, I was loth to see all the fine pipe tobaccos given away, so I wrote home, requesting a briar. After its arrival, and with my charpoy side-table stacked high with Navy Cut, I made smoke-screens wherever I went.

The officers and men of the 2nd Welch were still suffering from war-weariness and debilitation and, as there was no reason for the battalion to remain in hot and humid Toungoo, we decamped into the mountains, to the township of Taung-gyi. It proved to be the nearest place to paradise on earth. At 5,400 feet, the plateau basked under a clear, blue sky for most of the year, with a day temperature comparable to the best of a British summer. There were ground frosts on some nights and the monsoon, when it came, was nothing more than a fine mist and a gentle drizzle. We were in the Shan States to the east of Burma, and the Shan people were of a gentle, peaceful nature and gave us a warm welcome. Following long occupation by the Japanese, our presence signified a return to normality. In pre-war times a British Resident had occupied the Residency building in the town for very many years. Prior to the Japanese invasion and occupation, he had been a Lieutenant Colonel Stansfield, and the high regard he commanded from the populace is best illustrated by what he told me on his return to Taung-gyi. During his term of office he had acquired many items of value, mainly because the town was on the main trade route east to west. He had collected beautiful rugs, carpets, fine bone-china, precious stones, silks and jewellery of gold and silver. The Japs had overrun the country with unexpected ease and the Colonel was forced to flee, leaving behind everything except for a few easily carried valuables. When he returned to Taung-gyi he found the Residency bare, but for a few sticks of furniture. Within an hour a steady stream of locals came up the drive, each carrying one or more of his prized possessions. The locals had raided the house before the Japs arrived, taken everything of value, to hide and await the Colonel's return. It says much for their confidence in a British victory and for their simple love and honesty.

Coincidental with our battalion's move to Taung-gyi, I was invited to accept the position of IO (Intelligence Officer) at Brigade HQ under Brigadier 'Jumbo' Morris. It was a move I shall never regret, for it was the key to some remarkable experiences.

The first involved a party of fifty or sixty Japanese soldiers who wished to surrender. Weeks after the war ended there were still groups of them wandering about the countryside with nowhere to go, living off the land and in desperate straits. This bunch were reported to be a day's journey away and it fell to my lot as IO to go and collect them, while others quickly constructed a POW (prisoner of war) camp from the inevitable bamboo. Early one morning I assembled twelve jeeps and trailers with Indian Army drivers, enough rations for three days and, with Hynes by my side, we set off in the general direction of Thailand. In late afternoon we arrived at the deserted village where the Japs were reported to be, to find that they had left.

As we sat around, eating our curry and *chapatis*, an officer from the guerilla Force 136 appeared and informed me that our Japs had given themselves up to some other Allied forces further south. He then disappeared as mysteriously as he had come. I decided that our best course was to make camp in the village overnight and set out back to HQ the following morning. It was dusk when, out of the gloom, emerged a large elderly lady dressed in a nun's flowing habit. I had, I thought, grown accustomed to strange events in the Far East but this, well! I recovered my composure while Hynes still stared goggle-eyed at the apparition in the diminishing light. As for the Indians, they weren't sure whether to prostrate themselves, or melt into the background. Madam nun recognised my rank, assumed I was running the show and came over. We shook hands and sat cross-legged on the ground. She told me that there was a nunnery in the village and asked very politely whither we were bound. I explained the situation and told her that we were heading back to Taung-gyi first thing in the morning. Her eyes lit up at this news, and she asked if we would convey her and some other nuns to the main convent in Kalaw, a township just a few miles beyond Taung-gyi. With no Japs to ferry, I acceded willingly to her request, and it was arranged that our convoy would turn up at her establishment at 09.00 hours the following morning. With that she went. I lit a last pipe, Hynes and I played a game of crib then repaired to our mosquito-netted beds for the night.

The following morning after breakfast we drove to the nunnery and found a large building with a courtyard. It had a circular lawn with a drive around it, and it was just long enough to accommodate all the jeeps and trailers in line. Two nuns appeared, one bearing a glass jug full of a pale liquid, and the other, a cracked tumbler. I was invited to partake and, not wishing to offend, I accepted. Nun Number One poured out a full tumbler. I took a large swallow and, through my tears, said how very nice it was. I was drinking unsweetened lemon juice, with added salt as a substitute for the sugar that they hadn't seen for many moons. It is to my eternal credit that I drank the lot! The welcoming ceremony over, I indicated my wish to get moving and both nuns re-entered the building.

A few minutes passed before our passengers emerged, and then the sight that met our eyes rooted us to the spot. There came upon us six nuns and about twenty children of assorted sexes and ages, ranging from babes-in-arms to seven- or eight-year-olds. The kids sat on the grass while the nuns went back into the building and kept reappearing with an astonishing array of equipment. There were bags, beds, cots, mattresses, potties – enamel, babes-for-the-use-of, sheets, blankets – you name it, they brought it. We distributed the stuff between the jeeps, tied the cots on top, squeezed the kids and my escorting soldiers in as best we could, and seated the nuns in the rear seats. And then the oddest army convoy ever witnessed set course for Kalaw. I drove the leading jeep, with Hynes by my side and two nuns in the rear, both nursing tiny tots. The nun behind me was Italian, and in good English she unfolded their tale. The children in their care were orphans, whose parents had mysteriously disappeared during the Jap occupation. They had eaten little for weeks and they saw us as saviours, sent from The Lord in answer to their prayers.

Indeed, the Good Lord did smile on us, otherwise all six of us in the leading jeep would have joined Him long before we'd reached our destination. The monsoon had left the road in a deplorable state. Deep ruts and potholes made for slow progress in the wooded mountains and, as we rounded a bend, the side of the road gave way, leaving our offside front wheel dangling over a sheer drop of several hundred feet. Hynes made to leap out to help and I grabbed his arm in the nick of time. We were delicately balanced on the edge of the precipice and Hynes' departure would have tipped the balance and sent us hurtling into the abyss. The two nuns remained silent and calm. Our Indian *naik* (corporal) came alongside, sized up the situation, had a word, brought another jeep up, attached ours to it and, pulling hard at an angle of 45°, towed us to safety. It had been a close encounter of the nasty kind.

As we passed through Taung-gyi, we were cheered to the echo, and again in Kalaw, until we were met and welcomed at the convent by the Mother Superior. She invited me in for refreshment, which I declined gracefully, fearful that I might again be subjected to the torture of salted lemon juice. We departed with sincere thanks ringing in our ears and prayers enough to guarantee our entry at the Pearly Gates. Strange and unexpected our convoy may have been, but the payload we carried was in every way sweeter than the gaggle of Japs we had anticipated.

However, our construction of the POW stockade was not in vain. A party of about sixty prisoners did arrive, under the command of a Japanese WO (Warrant Officer). They came in the gloaming and I ushered them into the enclosure, told the WO that I would be back at 09.00 hours in the morning and shut the gate. There was no lock, it wasn't necessary. They were thousands of miles and an ocean away from their homeland, with no choice but to await repatriation. Promptly at

09.00 hours the following morning I opened the gate and there they were, in three ranks, with the WO in charge. As I entered, he uttered a word of command and, as one, they all fell flat on their faces in the dust. The WO gave me a smart salute and waited. With the war barely over, I must now be honest and confess that, at the time I had hatred in my heart for every buck-toothed, slit-eyed Jap that drew breath. I had fought them, they had made attempts on my life and had killed my friends, and here they were, on a sun-kissed morning at my mercy. I could have shot the whole bloody lot of them, but compassion for a half-starved, beaten enemy prevailed. I ordered the WO to stand at ease, to bring his men to their feet and to dismiss them to their quarters. I further told him that I would inspect them daily in their quarters and that all I expected was for them to stand to attention, as my own men did when I entered their living accommodation. During their stay we fed them, provided medical attention as required and treated them like fellow human beings, which is more than they did for the prisoners they took.

Towards the end of 1945 or early in 1946, the powers-that-be decreed that the 14th Army should celebrate a notable victory by holding a celebratory tattoo in the Burmese capital city of Rangoon. It was also rightly decided that pride of place should be allocated to the Burmese rulers and dignitaries who, by and large, had been uncooperative to the Japanese and who had proffered us their collaboration, as and when it became possible. Taung-gyi was in the State of Yaungwhe and, in my capacity as IO, I was ordered to make an appointment to call on the Sawbwa – the Shan equivalent of an Indian Maharajah.

An audience was granted, I went and presented my credentials at the palace and was ushered into his presence. He proved to be a kindly, benign, middle-aged gentleman and he accepted the invitation to the tattoo with obvious pleasure. He was without motorised transport, so we arranged that I would collect him at an appointed day and time and drive him the full day's journey to Rangoon.

The great day came. I arrived at the palace complete with

Hynes and two jeeps, with an Indian Army *havildar* (sergeant) driver for the second vehicle. I was ushered into a reception-cum-waiting room and attended to by the Sawbwa's third and youngest wife, who brought me a dainty cup of black coffee and a plate of sugary sweetmeats. When I had eaten, she returned, told me all was ready and led me back to the court-yard where our jeeps were parked. Through the portals came His Highness, escorted by his personal guard of four smart young men. They were dressed in loose black trousers and tunics piped in red, and they carried rifles so ancient that I doubt whether they could have slain a moth at point blank range.

We embussed and sallied forth and had hardly gone any distance when the following surprising conversation began. It went something like this:

Sawbwa: 'Where do you come from?'
Me: 'Britain, Sir.'
Sawbwa: 'Yes, I know, but from what part of the country?'
Me: 'Well it's a bit to the west of England, called Wales.'
Sawbwa: 'I thought so – anywhere near Swansea?'

You could have knocked me down with a sheet of toilet paper! How on earth was this royal personage from the Shan hin-terland acquainted with Swansea? An explanation was forth-coming: he had interests in oil. Swansea was and is synonymous with oil-refining, and, even as we drove, his second son was attending Swansea University. From that moment we were firm friends. The tattoo was a great success and my new-found friend enjoyed it all immensely, as did I. When it came to an end, I escorted him back to his palace, was treated to a second lot of coffee and sweeties and, in due course, I received a very nice letter expressing his gratitude for my company and felicitous attendance and that was it, or so I thought.

Some time later I received a printed invitation card to a Yaungwhe Festival Of The Lake. I was to be the Sawbwa's guest for two days, with accommodation provided in one of his guest-houses. I had no inkling of what to expect and, even if I had, the events that unfolded were beyond any westerner's imagination. The Shans pay homage to Buddha and the per-sonification of Yaungwhe's deity was perched on a huge, float-ing platform anchored in the middle of a lake so vast, that it looked more like a sea than an inland stretch of fresh water – so vast, that it made Wales's largest lake in Bala resemble a garden pool. The massive Buddha spent fifty-one weeks of the year floating placidly on the waters, from whence He cast His benign influence over all of Yaungwhe. It is believed that He ensures the peace and prosperity of this idyllic land and, as a token of the people's gratitude, respect and devotion, He is brought from the lake into their midst for a week-long period of festive worship once a year.

It was the manner of His move that proved both exciting and intriguing. On the morning of the great day, hordes of people gathered on the wood-planked quayside. It was a happy and colourful scene. Under a crystal-clear blue sky the peach-complexioned, soft-skinned Shan women wore bodices of pure white above wrap-around skirts of all colours, and the majority carried open multicoloured parasols, to add to the gaiety of the occasion. Moored in the water were a number of very long, narrow boats, each hewn and fashioned from a single tree-trunk. Down the centre of each and along its entire length ran a bamboo pole at waist height, supported by a bamboo post at each end. Each boat was crewed by twelve lithe and lusty young men, six on each side of the pole, standing and holding on to it with one hand. In the other they held an oar, about six to eight feet in length, which passed between their legs and into the water. Finally, in the centre of each craft sat the cox, cross-legged, and in front of him, suspended from the bamboo pole, hung a brass gong. The boats were in line abreast and at the crack of a rifle, they were off like hares out of a trap. The oarsmen rowed with their arms and legs, synchronising their movements with the pulsating beat of the gong. The light craft cut through the water at a speed that would have left Oxford and Cambridge crews wallowing in their wake. It was a race in deadly earnest. The prize for the first boat to reach the Buddha was the privilege and honour of being in 'pole-position' on the return journey. On attaining their goal, each boat tied up to the deity's platform and, to the throb of the lead boat's gong, towed 'The Great God Bud' back to the expectant throne on the quayside. I was accorded the privilege of accompanying the boat race in a guest craft which, I think also carried a referee to see fair play. There was then much feasting, and that is an understatement. Intoxicating beverages appeared at my side as if by magic, and I'm afraid my recollections of the remaining hours are wreathed in an alcoholic haze.

Those days in the Shan States were wonderful and memorable, a paradise on earth, but, regrettably, every paradise has its resident snake. In Taung-gyi, it was the rat. When the rains came and there were no crops to plunder, the rodents deserted the countryside and headed for the towns and villages. Their presence was bad enough, but to make matters worse they carried the deadly bubonic plague. We had been warned, and at the sight of the first rat all ranks were injected with anti-plague serum. I had previously been inoculated against typhoid, tetanus and cholera, with no ill-effect. This was different. Following our jabs, we took to our beds for a day of deep and desperate depression. Of course we recovered, and not one of us was smitten with the dreaded disease.

Once again, gardening entered my life in that far-flung 'Nirvana' of the Orient. Brigadier 'Jumbo' Morris was a keen gardener like myself, and asked me to pen an air mail letter to Suttons, requesting a seed catalogue. It duly arrived and together he and I held a mini horticultural meeting, and made out an order for a selection of vegetable seeds, which I mailed. The parcel came and the seeds were sown in a patch of ground not far from the mess. In the near-perfect climate, germination was good and growth was rapid, and a succession of fresh, familiar vegetables were harvested and consumed with relish. As one crop matured, we sowed another and then another. There seemed no end to the earth's fertility and bounty, helped along by an unlimited supply of manure from several sources, including water buffalo.

We loved the good life and were rapidly restored to health and fitness. Our Indian cook was equally adept at preparing both delicious curries and good, wholesome British dishes and 'booze' suddenly became plentiful and cheap. Beer was rationed to a dozen cans a month, but they were supplemented by bottles of effervescent, American ale. The label on the bottles bore the name 'Lion', but the contents hadn't the strength of a kitten. Duty-free British gin and Scotch whisky cost the equivalent of about 5 shillings (25 pence) a bottle. The inevitable happened. With little to occupy our time, we all ate and drank to excess and organised frequent mess parties, ostensibly to celebrate victory. A party at the 4th/6th Gurkhas mess called for a strong constitution. They served 'Tiger's Milk' – a lethal concoction of goat's milk liberally laced with rum, and with the power to stun many a good man. When called upon to sing, I obliged with excerpts from Gilbert and Sullivan, 'Glorious Devon', 'Sospan Fach' and an aria or two with words that could never appear in print. Prender, the CO of the 3rd/6th Rajputana Rifles, a mountain of a man with the gait of a gazelle, regaled us with 'Frankie and Johnny', the only song he knew. He performed it superbly, but after hearing it umpteen times, it began to pall a bit!

We officers at HQ were a mixed bunch, drawn from the various units that constituted 62 Brigade. One was a chubby faced young lieutenant from the Gurkhas. His orderly had never been known to smile until the night of one of our mess parties. His officer imbibed over-well and swayed out of the mess on his way back to his tent. Our HQ had previously been occupied by the Japanese, who had dug a number of trench latrines in the area. They were disguised with a cover of bamboo matting and our inebriated friend stepped on one of them and fell in. His normally expressionless orderly broke into spasms of uncontrollable mirth.

The Gurkhas are the finest body of soldiers in the world and their loyalty and devotion to their officers is legendary. I call to mind one example of many: our BM (Brigade Major) Major John Ricketts and his orderly, nicknamed the 'Frog' because he was so bow-legged that one could drive a rickshaw between his legs, had been man, servant and firm friends through unspeakable hardships. Shortly before I joined Brigade HQ, John had left for home. The Frog was left high and dry and, for some reason, took to running errands for me. One morning he came to my room in a state of intense excitement, holding a small parcel which he handed to me with the request that I open it. This I did, to find inside a case containing a beautiful gold wristwatch and a note from Major Ricketts addressed to his Frog. In essence, the major expressed his heartfelt thanks for his servant's unshakeable love and loyalty and asked him to accept the timepiece as a gift. As I read the note out to him, tears streamed down the Frog's face, and when I'd finished he asked me to wind the watch and set it to the correct time. I did so, explaining the simple procedure as I went along, and then I made to put it on his wrist. He took a quick step backwards, telling me that as the watch was from his beloved Major *Sahib*, he was not fit to touch it. I replaced it in its case and handed it to him, and he took it as though it was a piece of priceless china. For the remainder of the time I spent at HQ he sought me out daily to wind his wristwatch, while he gazed at it adoringly.

The peace brought regular letters from my Glen and sometimes photographs of our baby daughter. Most of us proudly displayed photographs of our offspring on our bedside tables with considerable pride, even though some of us had never seen our sons and daughters. Then someone had the bright idea of holding a photographic 'beautiful baby' competition. The 2nd Welch joined in the fun and, from dozens of entrants, my lovely baby daughter won first prize – six cans of Felinfoel's best bitter. A sergeant's baby boy was voted the ugliest infant on show and won a bottle of Scotch for his dad as compensation.

Glen felt terribly alone when the glad news came through that Germany had fallen. On VE night in our village, as everywhere else, there was great rejoicing. The church bells rang out, blackout material was torn down, the lights shone forth and there was dancing and feasting in the streets. As it happened, I was the only village boy on the Burma front, still at war. How she envied her neighbours' revelry, especially since overseas mail had been delayed and she had heard nothing from me for six weeks.

General 'Pete' Rees, commanding 19th Division had departed on a home posting, to be replaced by General P. C. Marinden. He was a tough, wiry little man who had spent much of his war commanding marauding infantry units behind enemy lines. He joined the division without his ADC, (Aide de Camp) and inexplicably invited me to fill the vacancy. I liked him and felt pleased and privileged to join his staff. Once more I found myself back in Toungoo where the Divisional HQ was based, and during the few months we were together the General and I became firm friends. I helped run his daily life, making sure he kept his appointments, attending parades and inspections and driving him around in an 'acquired' staff car. It had been found, virtually and surprisingly intact, in an abandoned Jap transport dump and, as it was a sleek, smart Lincoln Zephyr, it became 'General Marinden's – for-the-use-of'. Someone made a Divisional pennant to fly on the bonnet and we travelled around in style.

During the few months of my tenure as ADC there were two incidents that I remember well. The first resulted from an invitation to the General from the ruler of Kentung on the Burma/Indo-China border to pay his respects, when it became known that he was to visit a Company of Gurkhas in the area. We were lodged in a luxurious guest-house, waited on hand and foot and served with sumptuous meals. On the table stood a beautiful hand-carved fruitbowl with an intricate design in gold on black-lacquered wood. Our admiration of the superb work of art was noted and in the morning we were invited to accompany a guide who would conduct us to the bowl maker. We travelled some miles by jeep, then walked a mile or two along a narrow woodland path until we came upon a bamboo hut. Outside squatted a wizened Shan in front of a charcoal fire, on which a black, viscous liquid bubbled in a small metal pan. When we arrived, the little chap was beating wafer-thin gold-leaf to a powder and at his side was a half-finished vase. The only visible tools of his trade were the hammer he used for assaulting the gold-leaf and a well-worn, razor-sharp pen-knife. With nothing more than these simple implements, this artistic genius fashioned some of the loveliest *objets d'art* I have ever seen.

Through our guide we enquired whether we could purchase some of his masterpieces. He concurred, but regretted that there were only two that were finished and saleable. Naturally, the General had first choice and bought an ornate bowl, leaving me with a plaque depicting six warriors in tribal dress. I still have it, and on the back is a circle of gold paint inscribed in Shan lettering. Some day I may come across a Shan Statesman who can decipher the words for me.

Shortly after, Divisional HQ left Toungoo in convoy for Rangoon, to board a ship bound for Calcutta. It was the beginning of the end, and I viewed it with mixed feelings. Both Hynes and I knew we were a step nearer home, but it tore at our heartstrings to part with so many officers and men with whom we had shared so many experiences. It was also sad to see the slow disintegration of a Division that had fought with honour and valour for so long.

The other memorable incident occurred as we reached the outskirts of Rangoon on the very first day of the monsoon rains. The sun broke through the clouds and I stopped the car at a streetside water hydrant, where three or four youngsters appeared to be filling their buckets with water. I approached them, to ask the way to the city centre. Without a word, they all threw the contents of their buckets over me. Soaked to the skin, I grabbed a full bucket and retaliated. Hynes joined in the fun and for a few minutes we fought a losing water-battle against the grinning, yelling youths. Finally, peace was declared and they gave us the directions we sought. Unknowingly, we had been participants in the annual so-called Water

Festival, celebrating the advent of the rains and the end of the months of drought when every drop of water had to be carefully conserved.

Within a few days our much depleted Divisional HQ was on board ship, heading for Calcutta, and for a very short while the General and I stayed at that city's most prestigious hotel – Spence's. Normally, its paying guests qualified for admittance only if they held, at the very least, a Major's rank. I was a mere Captain but, as I was ADC to the General, I was allowed in. For the first time in months I slept between clean white sheets. I used a bathroom with all mod. cons., had the use of a billiard table and dined regally on the best fare that India could produce.

In those days in India poverty was rife and dire among the teeming lower classes. No one seemed to value life. One morning I walked across Chowringee Bridge and stepped around a woman's dead body lying on the pavement. Everyone else did likewise, and when I returned two hours later the corpse still lay where it had fallen. She had probably died of hunger, because no person or organisation thought fit to feed her. I saw a young mother with a fly-infested dead baby in her arms, begging for alms in a voice so weak that it foretold imminent death, and I saw a man suffering from elephantiasis, whose distended scrotum touched the ground as he shambled along. I saw many more such tragic human beings, condemned to suffering and deprivation by a caste system which decrees that the poor must remain poor in an uncaring society.

From Calcutta we moved by train to Lohardaga, a small village some forty or so miles from Ranchi. We established a tented camp outside the village walls and just sat there, waiting for something to happen. The only event that broke the endless monotony was an invitation to the General from the Maharajah of the small adjacent independent state of Jasphur Naga, to be his guest for a few days at a guest-house by a river where the fish were, reputedly, plentiful. I swam and frolicked in the clear waters. The General fished and didn't catch a thing.

At long last the General received his posting back to England and asked me to drive to Ranchi and buy him six pairs of lisle stockings as a gift for his mother; he was so grateful that he presented me with his fishing rod. With his departure, Divisional HQ disintegrated. My faithful Hynes was repatriated and I went back to Calcutta, this time to a transit camp and not to a plush hotel. It was August and Calcutta was insufferably hot, and so humid that one's clothing stuck to one's skin. The highlights of my days were breakfast, lunch, dinner and a strange ritual that occurred at 16.00 hours daily. A knock on my door heralded the arrival of a mess waiter, bearing a plate heaped with chips accompanied by a small bowl of Heinz tomato ketchup – very odd. I detested the place and, to make matters worse, I suffered my first bout of malaria. I firmly believe that I had taken my daily Mepacrin tablet regularly, but whether I had taken it or not, I had unmistakenly contracted the disease.

Thankfully, my repat papers arrived at last and at the end of August 1946 I boarded ship and bade farewell to India's shores. Compared with the SS *Windsor Castle*, the ship was a tub, but the food was good. During the voyage I made a few new friends and a Colonel's fourteen-year-old daughter fell in love with me. I resisted her innocence, and on a cold, rainswept morning in September, Liverpool's Liver Birds hove into view. We disembarked and I was back on British soil. At a demob unit in York I collected the necessary discharge papers, a demob suit and overcoat, wired Glen and caught a train to Carmarthen.

Home Sweet Home

ॐ

THE train journey took only a few hours; it felt like years. At last, in the day's fading light, the train pulled into Carmarthen and there on the platform stood my Glen. And then she was in my arms and the past blurred into oblivion. A hired car stood waiting. We sat in the back and hardly spoke a word during the hour-long journey to Aberporth. After such a long parting our hearts were too full for words. Being together was enough.

When the war in the Far East came to an end in August 1945, I had immediately reapplied for admission to the University College of Wales in Aberystwyth, to read botany, zoology and chemistry with the intention of graduating in botany. My original application, submitted before I was enlisted into the Armed Services, had been accepted and I felt confident that the college authorities would view my request sympathetically. I was delighted when they did.

It was through Glen's efforts and the good offices of our Liberal Member of Parliament that I secured my early Class B release from the Army, in time to attend the first college term in October 1946. As soon as Glen knew the approximate time of my return, she had begun her search for a suitable home for the three of us in Aber. Fortune smiled on her and she procured a second-floor flat in Chalybeate Street in the town centre. It comprised a tiny kitchen, a sitting-room, one large and one small bedroom and a small bathroom. The only lavatory served all the building's occupants and stood on a landing between the first- and second-floor flats. The ground floor was occupied by a ladies' drapery emporium, run by widowed Mrs Rees, and the top floor housed an asthmatic, middle-aged lady and her young daughter. The whole outfit was owned by the Harries, bachelor brothers who lived in style in a large house on the promenade. We were granted tenancy of the flat for the princely sum of 12/6 (65½ pence) a week.

Glen had found a place that was to be our home for five years and, with the enthusiastic support of both our families, she furnished it. In those immediate post-war years, all items of furniture were 'utility' grade and could only be purchased by the presentation of the appropriate number of dockets. By pooling all their resources, our families were able to purchase a bedroom suite and a lounge suite. The kitchen furniture we scrounged from various members of the family and, as a result, we had our first home.

However, we did not occupy the flat immediately. During the first week following my return, we stayed with Glen's family and the first of my civvy-street problems reared its ugly head. On our first night together for nearly two years we slept in a double bed with Janice, our little girl, in a cot alongside. She awoke at her customary early hour to see a strange man in bed with her mother. My unannounced appearance had a traumatic effect on her. As far as she was concerned, I was an interloper who vied with her for her mother's love and affection. She rejected me completely and I, for my part, resented her rejection and subconsciously regarded her presence as an intrusion into the intimate one-to-one relationship Glen and I had previously enjoyed. I believe this is a problem shared by many young married couples when a baby arrives, and in our case my daughter was no longer a babe when she first set eyes on me. During those early months we came very close to hating each other, but as hate is akin to love and love is the stronger emotion, the passage of time healed our initial mutual dislike and fostered a deep love.

A few days before we left our home ground, I was invited to attend a Grand Concert in Blaenporth School as the community's guest of honour, a visible sign that I was welcomed back into its midst. The prime performers of the district sang and recited. There were speeches of welcome, couched in words that portrayed me in glowing colours. The evening ended with much feasting and a cheque for £5.00 from the local Forces Fund. And so Glen and I bade farewell to our birthplace, its golden beaches and golden-hearted people, and established our first home in Aberystwyth. I duly registered as a student at the college and embarked on my studies.

In the late forties and early fifties the majority of the students were ex-servicemen and women, and many found it extremely difficult to adjust to civilian and student life. We had come through hell and high water and there was no one to counsel us, to ease us from trauma to tranquillity. Also, many of us had lived for years in a totally male society – and, as an army officer, practically everyone had been at my beck and call. My room had been cleaned, my uniform pressed and laid out, my boots and shoes polished, my food prepared and every evening after dinner we had gathered in the mess, smoked, talked, played cards and downed our beers and *chota pegs*, (spirits). We'd been spoiled rotten. The transition to a new life was extremely difficult, and it was many months before some of us found our civilian identities. In the interim we wasted our evenings in The Skinner's Arms, The Farmer's Arms, The Cooper's Arms and other alcoholic arms that gladly separated us from our hard-won gratuities and grants.

Glen accepted and suffered my initial refusal to face this new life with astonishing tolerance. Our saving grace, I believe, was the fact that we had known each other from childhood, and she must have been aware that under the skin of her less than considerate, boozing husband, lay the youth she once knew, latent but not dead. It was the Rag Ball of 1947 that came to our rescue. I bought her a slinky, green gown, complete with a red rose below the shoulder, and my lovely wife was the belle of the ball. It was not surprising that a month or so later it became evident that she was once again with child and on the seventeenth of November our son Richard joined the family. I believe he was the first child to be sired by a student (legitimately) in the college's history and there was great rejoicing among both staff and students. Within twenty-four hours Glen's hospital room resembled a florist's shop and there was a constant stream of visitors and congratulatory cards and telegrams.

Initially, our son was not a pretty sight. He was the colour of an overripe raspberry, his face bore the wrinkles of an octogenarian and his head seemed to have passed through a mangle. But he was our son and I loved him deeply on sight. With care and attention and the application of appropriate and adequate nutrients, my seedling son developed into a handsome adult. I am forever in his debt, because his birth brought me to my senses and concentrated my thoughts on my family, rather than on the past and on myself. My love for him was reciprocated manyfold and Janice, witnessing the relationship, came to the conclusion that I must be her father also and offered me her love, which I gladly returned. At last we were a family. This experience confirmed my belief that the family is the cornerstone of civilisation, the foundation of a stable, caring society and the only hope for future generations.

Sadly, my new-found peace and happiness were soon to be shattered. A few weeks before the end of year examinations, as I attended a lecture, I began to shake and shiver uncontrollably. The dreaded malaria had returned. Back in our flat, I tried to convince Glen that I wasn't about to expire and took to my bed with two hot water bottles, where I continued to quiver like an aspen leaf in a gale. My temperature rose to giddy heights, steam rose from the bedclothes and still I shivered. The fever passed, leaving me as weak as lager, and when I had regained my strength I paid my doctor a visit. Not being conversant with tropical diseases, he prescribed the age-old remedy, quinine tablets, with the instruction that I should take one at the first sign of an attack. A month passed before it came, I swallowed a tablet and still sweated and shook, but the attack was over fairly quickly. Then they began to occur more frequently and on medical advice I took one quinine tablet daily. At first all went well, but gradually the attacks returned with increasing frequency and, to cap it all, the continuous dosages of quinine were playing havoc with my nervous system. Sounds were amplified out of all proportion and I began to hallucinate during the attacks. To illustrate the tragic comedy of the situation, I remember one occasion when, in my mental derangement, I was speeding down a road, perched on top of a motorised chest-of-drawers with Princess Margaret navigating. It sounds crazy – was I going crazy? Well, maybe I was. There are two kinds of malaria – Benign Tertiary (BT) and Malignant Tertiary (MT) and my increasingly serious symptoms indicated the presence of the MT variety. Unless checked and cured, it develops into Black Water Fever – the kidneys cease to function and death is the end result. As if to confirm my self-diagnosis, I became violent during attacks and, on at least one occasion, Glen had to resort to the assistance of a male neighbour to pin me to the floor.

The situation was desperate. Then along came a stroke of luck. One day when I called at Taylor Lloyd's the chemist to collect my quinine tablets, the assistant, who was well aware of my worsening condition, asked me whether I was prepared to be a medical guinea-pig. As I had nothing to lose, I acquiesced, whereupon he produced a small, trial tin of Paludrin tablets that were new on the market. If I remember correctly, I was to take three tablets a day for three weeks and then one tablet daily until the tin was empty. This I did, and from that day to this I have never suffered a single attack of malaria. I have to thank God and the Aber chemist's assistant for my life.

Lily Newton, the Professor of Botany at the University at the time, knew of my physical handicap and, bless her, made every effort to ensure my academic future. I was allowed to resit my examinations, but even with her help, I lost a year. However, a sympathetic Government renewed my grant. By my final year I had dropped chemistry and was reading botany and zoology, and with health on my side I tackled the exams with reasonable confidence. The botany papers, both theory and practical, went well and I thought that I had done quite well in zoology theory. But I hadn't counted on the perversity of one of the lecturers who was responsible for deciding on the specimen we were to dissect, draw and label for our practical test. I walked into the lab, and there on my dissection board lay an animal I had never seen before. I knew I was beaten before I'd begun and, together with other ex-service students, I walked out. I learnt later that the damned thing was a salamander. There was no way I could have exposed and identified the creature's innards and, at that moment, I could have cheerfully dissected the lecturer. I was in trouble and I knew it.

It was then that Professor Newton came to my rescue. Up on Penglais Hill above the town, the embryonic stages of a new college were taking shape, adjacent to The Welsh Plant Breeding Station and The National Library of Wales. Across the road stood the Principal's new abode, set in several acres of farmland destined to become the Botany Garden. A head gardener had been appointed and, together with a fellow salamander-sufferer, Lily Newton offered me a job as an assistant gardener-cum-labourer at £4 7s. 6d. (£4.37½) a week. I leapt at the chance and also took her advice to take a crash course in economics to complete my degree course. It was one of the best moves I have ever made.

My year at Penglais has since proved invaluable. On my first day there was nothing except a trio of interlinked greenhouses, a potting shed and a boiler house in the course of construction. It wasn't much, but in the space of twelve short months, Penglais was transformed. To begin with, we concentrated on the greenhouses, designating one a tropical house, the second frost-free and the third a cold house. When they were ready, the plants arrived in their hundreds and it fell to my lot to write their labels, and there is no better way of learning about plants and their identities. We planted trees and shrubs by the score, cleared acres of ground, sowed a massive lawn and created our *pièce de résistance* – a large rock garden.

It was during the construction of this rockery that I very

nearly killed the head gardener. Load after load of massive boulders were delivered and it took two strong men and much heaving to set even the smallest in its proper place in the rockery. The largest boulders were immovable but, fortunately, they were grained and, providing a cold chisel was positioned in the right place, they could be split into one or more manageable chunks. I was taller and stronger than the head gardener, so he opted to hold the chisel while I took mighty swipes at it. All went well until we came to tackle a particularly large boulder. We found the split line, the chisel was positioned, I lifted the sledge hammer and with all the power I could muster, I swung it. My aim was true, but halfway through its arc of descent, the hammer head flew off and sped past the head gardener's left ear with only an inch or two to spare.

There and then I learnt an invaluable lesson. Accidents can happen, even in the peaceful pursuit of gardening, and it pays to handle tools and equipment with care and respect. It says much for the head gardener's faith and stoicism that, after replacing the hammer head securely back on to its handle, he continued to hold the chisel, although I couldn't fail to notice that he closed his eyes before I took a swipe at it.

£4. 7s. 6d. a week in those days was enough to live on, and I supplemented my pay by stoking the boiler at nights and weekends and also by serving two nights a week behind the lounge bar of The Talbot Hotel. Life, it seemed to me, was good, very good. I was gardening in earnest, we were among true friends and as a family we enjoyed the summers on Aber's beaches. I was contemplating a second year at Penglais when I learnt that a local family was looking for a gardener to care for their three-acre garden on the outskirts of the town. I got the job and we moved from the flat to the estate's lodge. Once again I'd made a good move. My new boss was a widow with a wealth of gardening knowledge, and she liked nothing better than to spend time working with me and talking about the plants she knew and loved. It was invaluable experience and my horticultural know-how advanced by leaps and bounds.

Prior to my year at the Botanic Gardens, I had suffered

withdrawal symptoms. Our town flat had no garden and I felt the frustration of being isolated from the natural world and being deprived of the joy of growing things and the feel of fertile soil on my hands. I tried to fill the void. Our flat had five wide window ledges that caught the morning sun, and all I needed were containers and soil to satisfy my craving for plants and colour. From our friendly greengrocer I obtained enough wooden tomato boxes to fill the ledges and, to disguise their origins, I painted them blue. From the same source I acquired a large sack and, armed with a small coal shovel and a bucket, I leapt on my bike and headed out of town. I soon found what I was looking for – a field full of sheep and mole-hills. I spent a pleasant couple of hours shovelling molehill soil into the sack and sheep droppings into the bucket, together with a few nice dry cowpats that were lying around. Then I loaded the stuff on the bike, pushed it back home, emptied and mixed the raw material in the tiny backyard, filled the tomato boxes and sowed the whole lot with nasturtium seeds. They germinated and grew, and thereafter our summer window-sills were a cascade of colour. In spring the boxes sprouted crocus and King Alfred daffodils, and their brilliance brought a splash of colour to the drabness of brick and concrete. Maybe it wasn't much, but it went some way to satisfy an inherent gardener's instinct to propagate plants and beauty.

That instinct is inherent in most of us, as I discovered in Liverpool a few years later. I was in the large Woolworth's store in Church Street, holding a gardening clinic behind the seed counter (they still had counters in those days). A queue formed and at the back stood a little elderly lady clutching a rose bush she had just purchased in the store. When, eventually, she reached me, her words were, 'Have you got any soil?' I pointed our that Woolworth's didn't sell soil and, anyway, didn't she have soil in her garden? 'No,' she said, 'because I haven't got a garden.' I was nonplussed. I enquired where she intended to plant the rose bush. She explained – her husband had removed a cracked lavatory pan; she had painted it green and put it on the brick-based backyard, outside her back door.

I rallied. Here was a kindred spirit with an insatiable urge to garden where no garden existed. Resisting the temptation to ask her whether she wanted 'a flush of bloom', I gently advised against the rose bush and, with the concurrence of the store manager, gave her a bag of compost, three geraniums and half a dozen lobelias. With thanks on her lips and a song in her heart, she scurried away and I hope, lived happily ever after.

In 1951 I was a very contented individual. I'd obtained my B.Sc., we were a happy family, living in the lodge, and I loved my work, tending a beautiful garden. I had slipped into a placid, pleasurable way of life and saw no reason for change, but Glen had other ideas. I have never been motivated by ambition, but she knew that whatever potential I might have would remain forever dormant unless I was pushed up life's ladder. Seeds and their mysteries have always intrigued me and, for no other reason than that, I wrote to Bees Ltd, of Liverpool, asking if they had a vacancy for a trainee seedsman. To my surprise, I received a reply by return, inviting me to attend for an interview.

The portents were not good. I caught the 7 a.m. train from Aberystwyth and arrived in Gobowen in a blizzard. My Liverpool connection was held up in the snow and it became apparent that I could not reach my destination in time for the interview. I rang the company, explained my predicament and they kindly rearranged our meeting for the following morning and told me to stay overnight at The Queen's Hotel, at the company's expense. The upshot of it all was that I was accepted for the post of trainee manager in the seed department, at a salary of £500 a year. My career in horticulture was under way and our dalliance in Aberystwyth was doomed.

We were sorry to leave Aber where we had had our first family home. It was there that I had regained my health and sanity and found a new happiness, and I knew that I would miss the many blissful days that my wife, the children and I spent on the beach and in the sea. I knew too that life would be poorer without the friends we had made in the town and in the college. But I would have good memories and there were many of those.

One such memory is of our early days, when Glen was a learner cook and when, spooning boiled potatoes out of a saucepan, a sodden dishcloth came out with them! She learnt quickly and has since mastered the culinary art to perfection, but until she did, we dined out in Aber's cafés and fish and chips from 'Johnny's' were regularly on the menu.

I also remember a certain professor, small of stature, who shall be nameless. He caught the evening train from Aber every Friday and returned on the last train on Sunday. No one knew where he went, but it was said that he had an illegitimate child in every town and village in Wales that boasted a station! And I remember one zoology lecture that has given me pause for reflection many, many times since. The professor took all the lectures on the subject of reptiles, tracing their history and evolution from prehistoric times to the present day. In his final lecture, he explained the extinction of the massive dinosaurs and their equally large co-dwellers, by indicating that they became over-evolved and over-specialised. In a rich and lush environment they outgrew their capabilities and perished from over-indulgence. On the other hand, the crocodile had not evolved, but had remained much the same throughout the ages. He had not advanced, had made no progress up the evolutionary tree, yet he still dwelt among us. He left us with these words, 'What price progress?'

The Seeds of Success

&ə

I JOINED Bees Ltd in February 1952, leaving Glen and the children in Aberystwyth. It is said that 'parting is such sweet sorrow', but as far as I was concerned, it was all sorrow without a soupçon of sweetness.

The company had arranged digs for me with a homely, elderly couple, a short bus journey from the seed factory. They were very nice people, but unfortunately Mrs Jones was an inexpert cook. Her cabbage was so overboiled that it was practically drinkable and her gravy was pure liquid fat. Sunday lunch was a weekly disaster. At twelve noon precisely, Mr Jones went to his local pub and, being a kindly soul, insisted that I went with him and, not wishing to offend, I did. As we left the house, his wife's words rang in our ears – 'Dinner will be ready at one. Don't be late.' Every Sunday Mr Jones replied, 'no, dear' and every Sunday we arrived back an hour late at two o'clock, to be met by a silent, stony-faced Mrs Jones and a plateful of cold, congealed mess. I couldn't stand it, and after a month of suffering I sought the help of my colleagues.

I was soon housed in an attic room in a beautiful house in Meols in the Wirral. My landlady was a charming, unmarried woman who kept lodgers more for company than for profit and she was a superb cook. I ate well, there was a large garden that I could potter around in, I could escape Liverpool's polluted air and I had interesting company. My fellow lodgers were a commercial traveller and a widowed lady in her eighties, who was a permanent resident. Dinner was served promptly at seven and the repast was always hilarious. The

128

rep regaled us with unlikely tales of his travels and female conquests, but old Mrs Owen was the star of the show. Her eyesight was poor, but her vanity prevented her from wearing her spectacles in our presence. As a result, the food on her plate was a blur and she loaded her fork more by guesswork than be design. Watching her chasing peas around her plate was almost unbearable, but she more or less triumphed in the end, by which time my co-'digger' and I were on the coffee.

The firm of Bees Ltd was founded at the turn of the century by A. K. Bulley, a Liverpool cotton merchant and a keen horticulturist. He had a house and many acres of land at Ness in the Wirral and there he created the still-renowned Ness Gardens, which were donated to Liverpool University by his daughter after his death. In his enthusiasm, he financed plant and seed collecting expeditions for Far Eastern countries and, even now, visitors to the garden will see the original plant of *Pieris forrestii*, sent back from China in 1906 by the great plant collector, George Forrest. He also bought approximately one thousand acres of land at Sealand near Chester, where he established a farm, a market garden and a massive nursery that grew and supplied all manner of plants to British gardeners. It was A.K.B.'s Company, hence the name Bees, and at one time it was the largest single horticultural enterprise in the country.

In Liverpool, the seed factory was an ill-planned, Dickensian-style madhouse. The tall, five-storey building plus basement stood on the corner of Mill Street in a rundown area of the city that, in 1952, still showed the scars of German bombing. I was made second-in-command of the seed-filling department, with the partial responsibility of ensuring that each machine achieved maximum output. The packeted seeds were despatched either to the thousand or so Woolworth's stores nationwide, or to the many thousand gardeners who ordered their seeds via the Bees catalogue. In those days, the slogan 'Bees – Seeds That Grow' was known in every household.

The Mill Street building was a manager's nightmare. The seed-filling department occupied the fourth floor. On the fifth floor were stacked sacks of fine seeds, with a further stock on the second floor. The office department was on the third floor and tons of peas and beans were stacked in the basement. I can honestly say that my first year in the seed industry was spent humping sacks of seeds in the company of Frank the foreman. He limped badly – the result of an earlier accident as a docker, and his breathing was laboured, but despite his disabilities he possessed the Liverpudlian's famous wit and there was never a dull moment in his company. Most of the seed packets were filled by machine and, in order to meet the filling schedule and subsequently process the orders, it was necessary to operate the machines at full capacity, five and a half days a week. Meeting the schedule would not have been difficult, except for one crippling, limiting factor – the building had only one lift. There was constant competition for its services, and pea and bean filling machines were frequently idle, as they waited for their raw material to be hauled up from the basement. It was the least efficient operation imaginable.

The top management comprised the Managing Director whom we seldom saw, although he occupied an incongruously plush office on the second floor. The office and seed department managers were two gnomes who appeared to be sworn enemies. My immediate superior was a wee Scotsman with a weakness for gin. Every morning, promptly at eleven o'clock, he emerged from his office, clutching a sheaf of papers and looking as though he was on his way to a crucial board meeting. He vanished down the rarely used, back stairs, came out into the street and scuttled into the pub on the corner. He repeated the process at one o'clock and again and two forty-five. Everyone knew the why and wherefores of his short trips, but he appeared to regard them as deadly secret. For all that, he was as efficient as the building allowed, and in a detached way we got on well together. The filling department was staffed entirely by young women, a hard-working bunch and soft-hearted under a veneer as hard as nails. Following a year of sack-humping, I was given complete charge of this 'harem', who regarded my soft-spoken ways and instructions with unveiled suspicion. A few were definitely uncooperative, and one in particular was especially cantankerous and outspoken. The vilest sergeant-major could have learnt from her unexpiated vocabulary and behind my back she would mutter unmentionable epithets that she knew I would overhear. I bore her acid tongue for some time until I finally snapped, rounded on her and 'tore her off a strip' that any trooper would have been proud of. From that moment I had the admiration and full cooperation of all the girls and production increased.

I was learning the horticultural seed trade very quickly. It came as a surprise to find that something like 80 per cent, at least, of all garden seeds were produced abroad in countries such as France, Holland, Denmark, New Zealand, Japan and the USA. As the flowers fade and the seeds form in the ovary, their vital need is for long periods of dry, sunny weather, conditions that are too uncertain in Britain to guarantee the production of seeds of high germination potential coupled with maximum longevity. I served the industry for twenty-nine years in various capacities and during that period I can assure gardeners that quality control throughout was of the highest standard.

The production of first-class seeds is a complex and highly-skilled operation and in 1956 I had the first of several opportunities to follow the process through from start to finish. I was sent to Denmark to visit three seed growers who conducted business with Bees Ltd. I stayed in five-star hotels as their guest and was collected by car every morning at 08.00 hours and taken to visit trial grounds and crops of flowers and vegetables grown from seed. On the first day the car drew up alongside a two-acre field which, under a cloudless blue sky, was a carpet of golden yellow. Countless Scotch marigolds were in full bloom, flaunting their petals in unashamed brilliance. We drove on to inspect acres of cauliflowers, cabbages and broccoli, all in bloom and ready to yield their seed crop at summer's end. Day after day I saw more, and more than enough to convince me that these were expert growers.

I am often asked to explain why seeds of F-hybrid varieties

of flowers and vegetables are comparatively expensive, and whether the extra cost is merited. An F-hybrid is the first-generation cross between two parents selected for their exemplary characteristics. The progeny should show typical hybrid vigour exemplified by strong growth, increased disease resistance and uniformity of performance. Unfortunately, seeds of F-hybrids themselves do not breed true, and only 50 per cent of the second generation display their parents' desirable attributes. Therefore the breeder and grower is compelled to backtrack and cross-pollinate from the original parent varieties year after year, an expensive and meticulous operation.

I cite just one example: At a seed grower's premises a few miles from Copenhagen, I was intrigued by a long row of small glasshouses, some of which housed onions in flower. The vents, though open, were covered by fine muslin and in each house stood a beehive. The bees were busy cross-pollinating the flowers, and all other external insects that could be carrying onion pollen from other onion varieties were denied access by the muslin. The hives were hired from local beekeepers who were on to a good thing. They were paid for the hire of the hives which they later recovered and harvested, selling the honey. Following harvest by the grower, all the seeds were laboratory tested for purity and germination and, the results proving satisfactory, were despatched to British and other seed retailers for packaging. At the retail end of the market samples are taken from all incoming consignments and subjected to further lab tests for purity and germination prior to packaging.

There is more. The British gardener is further protected from unscrupulous seed merchants by law. The Seeds Act 1920 decreed that all vegetable seeds with the exception of salads have to meet minimum, high-percentage germination and purity levels. Failure to comply leads to prosecution and a hefty fine. Seeds of salad vegetables were later included in the Act, which in turn has been superseded by equally stringent EEC regulations. At present, flower seeds are not subject to legislative control, but no reputable seed company in its right mind would risk its good name and future prosperity by offering substandard seeds for sale. British gardeners can buy their seeds secure in the knowledge that they will germinate, grow and thrive under the right conditions. Nevertheless, every seed company receives a number of 'failed germination' letters each year from its customers. Almost without exception, the failures were the customers' fault. They failed to fulfil the conditions necessary for germination, namely adequate moisture, warmth and aeration.

The seed industry has always been accident-prone and probably still is. I have never understood why women will take instruction in cooking and men will 'read all about it' before attempting to construct a kitchen cabinet, or tinker with a car engine, whilst the budding gardener will cheerfully sow and plant in the mistaken belief that Nature will do the rest. She will not. She expects the gardener to be conversant with the basic rules of gardening and to work alongside her, rather than ignore her outstretched, helping hand. It would help if gardeners read the instructions printed on the seed packet, but I'm afraid many do not.

I remember an occasion when I was conducting one of many gardening clinics in a Woolworth's store. A lady approached me and asked if we had any onion seeds. I led her to the seed rack, selected a packet and handed it to her. She handed it back and indicated that the seeds she was looking for were roughly the size of mothballs. What she wanted were onion sets, not seeds, so I found her a pack and she nodded her approval. Then she amazed me by asking whether I could guarantee that the sets would produce onions. I assured her that they would, whereupon she replied that the ones she had planted last year had produced leeks. I was lost for words! Had she made a discovery that would rock the horticultural world to its foundations? Mustering my reserves, I asked her to describe how she had planted them and all became clear. Ignoring the advice on the pack, she had planted them at least six inches deep with a trowel, when they should have been sitting on top of the soil. The poor things had struggled valiantly to the surface and believe it or not, she had even cooked them as leeks and proclaimed that they were quite nice. They say that, 'there's nowt as queer as folks' and I can prove it. I once sent a complimentary packet of carrot seeds to a lady, who returned it with an accompanying letter, to the effect that 'neither I nor my husband eat anything that grows below the ground.' I can't help thinking that their diet must be very limited. It takes strength of character and a vivid imagination to reply to gardening queries!

After spending just over a year with Bees, I was missing my family and began house-hunting in the Wallasey area, across the Mersey from Liverpool. My salary of £500 per annum limited my choice and I was fortunate to find a small semi in Wallasey village going for £1,100, an incredibly low asking price by today's standards. The external paintwork was non-existent and the interior needed decorating from top to bottom, otherwise it was in reasonably good condition. Somehow I found the £110 deposit and negotiated a 90 per cent mortgage at a barely affordable 10 per cent, but with strings attached. We could move in on payment of the deposit, but a proportion of the balance would be withheld for three months and would be paid to the vendors when I had painted all external wood-work. I agreed to the conditions but I had one more problem – no ladder. Our next-door neighbour, aware of our pre-dicament, told me that a nearby newsagent's had a ladder for hire at sixpence ($2\frac{1}{2}$ pence) per weekend. The seed factory worked on Saturday mornings and I was home by 2 p.m. and over at the newsagent's to collect the ladder by 2.30 p.m. Every Saturday afternoon and all day on Sundays I painted with feverish urgency and, with no time to spare, completed the task and finalised the sale.

My family, complete with Kim the corgi and our furniture from Aberystwyth, had moved in on payment of the deposit. It was immediately obvious that our bits and pieces were totally inadequate to furnish the house. There was just enough to equip the three bedrooms, the dining-room and the kitchen, leaving the sitting-room bare, and we were short of a dining-table. Ignoring mother's advice never to borrow, or buy anything I couldn't pay for, I purchased an oak drop-leaf table on hire-purchase for £16. Repayments were 5 shillings (25 pence) a week and I didn't feel happy until the debt was paid off, and that was the only time that I became an HP customer. For the first time in our married lives, I had a garden of my own, albeit a small one. Measuring approximately 15 feet by 18 feet, it had a narrow border at the far end and a pocket-handkerchief-sized lawn in the centre, which consisted mostly of daisies interspersed with a few blades of feeble grass. I cleared the weed-ridden border, planted a Mock Orange for colour and fragrance and a climbing rose and a few herbaceous perennials. I decided to resurrect the lawn which, though minute, was just big enough to lie on. It took no more than a few minutes to dig it, fertilise it, weed it, level it and sow it with grass seed. The seeds germinated quickly and from our dining-room window we looked out on a small, verdant, mini-meadow. The corgi liked it immensely, so much so that he dug it up and buried a bone in it!

In June of that year I was taken seriously ill with pneumonia and the local doctor was summoned. He was in a permanent alcoholic haze but technically sound, although psychologically a patient's worst enemy. When my fever was at its height, and in my wife's presence, I could hear him muttering, 'Hmm, he's pretty bad, but maybe he won't die.' Nevertheless, his ministrations restored me to health and, at the same time, nearly deprived us of a chicken dinner. Glen had bought a tender bird with the intention of producing a nourishing broth for her sick spouse and a good meal for herself and the children. The chicken happened to be in the kitchen sink, steeped in salt water, when the doctor turned up to check whether I was still breathing, and, if I was, to give me a further antibiotic injection. Glen boiled a kettle of water. He sterilised his needle, filled the syringe, stumbled and injected the lifeless chicken. As the bird was a luxury we could ill-afford to lose. Glen cooked it anyway, and we ate it on the assumption that it was, hopefully, healthier than when it was bought!

CLAY

The year we spent in Wallasey village was a difficult one for all of us. In Aberystwyth our two children had attended Welsh-speaking schools and we spoke Welsh in the home simply because it was our first language. The sudden transition to an English school was a traumatic experience for the children. Aged seven and five respectively, they found it extremely difficult to follow teaching in, what was to them, a foreign language. We immediately switched to speaking English at home and, children being adaptable, it wasn't long before they were communicating freely in their new-found tongue. Nevertheless, the transitional period was cruelly hard on them. They were the butt of their classmates' ragging and Janice was demoted to a lower class, which she took to be a reflection on her lack of intelligence. With her mother's help, she was back in the A form within one term.

Life was also financially difficult. With my weekly pay-packet holding approximately £9.50, there wasn't a penny to spare. By Thursday each week, Glen was down to her last sixpenny-piece, which was just enough to buy a pound of minced beef. She learnt to cook in a hard school and, despite our dearth of funds, she somehow managed to feed our family with good, wholesome meals. We lived within our meagre means and we were a very happy family. We loved each other, we had need of each other and that was enough.

I had served two years with Bees in Liverpool when the tide turned very much in our favour. The company had a second seed department at Sealand in Flintshire, a couple of miles from the Roman city of Chester. With the demand for packeted seeds at its peak in the post-war years, the company had outgrown its Liverpool premises and a large building had been purpose-built on Sealand's thousand acres. The manager of the Sealand seed unit was leaving and I was asked if I would like to step into his shoes. I didn't hesitate to accept for several reasons: firstly, the entire seed-filling operation was on ground level; secondly, there was a modern house on the estate that went with the job, and, thirdly, we could leave city and sub-urban life and return to the countryside – our natural element.

I also realised that the move would solve our financial problem. We put our house up for sale and immediately found a buyer who offered £1,300. The deal was clinched, so in little more than a year we had made a profit of £200, less expenses, and for the first time the red ink of my bank statements became cheerfully black. I bought an ancient sit-up-and-beg bicycle for a pound, to convey me the mile to and from my place of work and so that I could spend my lunch hour at home. There was a fair-sized garden at the back of the new house where I grew our own vegetables and fruit, although I needn't have bothered. The seed unit was adjacent to the market garden department and every Friday a large box of goodies was delivered to my office. There were tomatoes, mushrooms, cut flowers and anything else that happened to be in season. Such affluence following on deprivation was more than welcome. Also very welcome was the greater freedom enjoyed by the children. They had countless acres at their disposal and with their pals, they disappeared to catch tiddlers, build dens and things for hours at a time in complete safety.

We lived there for two idyllic years and I recall two events, one of which profoundly affected our lives. During the war and later in college, I had lost touch with my God. The cruelty and degradation of war had shaken my inborn blind faith and made me doubt an omnipotent power. In college my doubt magnified as the principles of Darwin's *Theory of Evolution* seemed to disprove the Old Testament writings. How could I collate the cavortings of Adam and Eve in Eden with the theory that Man is the last link in a chain of evolutionary events that began with a single-celled blob of an organism floating in a watery medium? These contradictions were coupled with the oft-asked question, 'if there is a loving God, why does He allow wars, killing, cruelty and similar Satanic acts?' I had no answer and took the easy way out, by putting them out of my mind.

So it was that for about ten years I rejected religion and did not attend a place of worship, although the children went to Sunday School with their friends. My cowardly indifference to the truth and to the meaning of life became evident when a trainee priest knocked on our door and was invited in. He was not long out of college, he was clear and sincere in his beliefs and he debated, rather than argued and, to cap it all, he was a very nice chap. He called frequently to enlighten my darkness and to tuck into Glen's superb cooking. As time passed, he put on weight and I began to find my way back into God's company. Rightly or wrongly, I now believe that the Old Testament is a work of fiction in part and a catalogue of fact in others. I believe that Adam and Eve, the serpent and the apple are figments of the imagination of scribes who were stuck for an opening chapter. As far as they knew, Man begat Man, therefore there had to be a man and a woman on the first day and, sinfully, they shared an apple and set the whole of humanity in motion. It was a logical explanation in its time, but belief in a supernatural God is illogical and its mystery can only be revealed in death. I can't say I have come to terms totally with the Theory of Evolution either. I must accept that plants and animals have evolved over a length of time beyond our conception. But, as I look around and see Earth's teeming life, its incredible beauty and its specialisation to match its environment, I cannot help but see the hand of God in every living thing. My answer to those who put the onus of blame for humanity's misdeeds on God is that our time on Earth is a privilege afforded us by a benign Almighty, and it is our responsibility and ours alone as to how we conduct ourselves. He does not interfere in our daily lives for good or evil and on the day of reckoning our deeds and misdeeds will be taken into account.

I enjoy life to the full and when the end is nigh I shall feel no fear – regret probably, but not fear. My grandmother died at the age of ninety-two and her passing was with dignity, peace and a touch of humour. She was not ill and she still possessed all her faculties, but she came to the conclusion that it was time she went. She took to her bed and two days before she died she summoned my mother and asked her to bring a bowl of warm water, soap and a face-cloth, because she was about to depart and wished to be presentable when she met her Maker. Mother complied with her wishes and took the necessaries up to Grandma's bedroom, to be told that she could take them back – 'I'm not going to die today, after all.' Two days later the process was repeated and in the evening Grandma passed peacefully away, saying that she could see her long deceased husband crossing a bridge to meet her with open arms. Death held no sting for her, nor does it for me.

The young, trainee curate in Sealand restored my faith in God. We attended his church and, in due course, Glen and I were confirmed into The Church In Wales by the Bishop of St Asaph. It was good to be back in God's family.

In the summer of 1956 we took a fortnight's holiday and we travelled in style. We could afford to hire a car, a gleaming black Morris Cowley and, for the first time in our married lives, Glen and I were relieved of the burden of hauling two children, the dog and our considerable bags and baggage on and off trains and buses. The children were beside themselves with excitement and so were Glen and I. The night before the momentous journey from Chester to Aberporth we pored over a road map, to determine the route we would take. After much discussion we opted for a journey that would take us through some of Wales's glorious countryside, passing through Llangollen and on to Bala, Dolgellau, over Plynlimon and headlong down to Aberystwyth.

The decision we took that evening was to change the course of our lives. We set off fairly early, passed through Wrexham and approached Llangollen in mid-morning. On the outskirts of the town we came upon what appeared to be a large warehouse, and seated on the steps outside were a number of girls and women dressed in green overalls. I remarked casually to Glen that they looked exactly like my seed girls at Sealand, who were similarly garbed. We drove through the town and stopped to admire the superb view in the valley of the Dee, with the river chuckling its way eastwards to within a mile of the house we had not long left. Only then did it dawn on me that the seed firm Cuthbert's had its headquarters in

Llangollen and that the green-clad damsels we had seen were probably seed packers, as indeed they turned out to be.

We had a wonderful holiday, but at the back of my mind a thought germinated and grew – wouldn't it be nice to live and work in the lovely wooded valley we had seen? I voiced my thoughts to Glen, who left me in no doubt that she was all for it. On our return home I wrote a letter to Cuthbert's Managing Director, itemising my qualifications and experience and enquiring whether there was a vacancy I could fill. Once again fate played a trump card. The company's young Production Manager had grazed his leg playing rugby and a few days later complained of headaches and a general lethargy. Despite medical attention his condition worsened, severe septicaemia was diagnosed and, being allergic to all known antibiotics, he died tragically and prematurely. I was the very man the company needed and, following an interview with the Chairman, I tended my resignation to Bees Ltd and joined Cuthbert's in February 1957 as Production Manager.

We moved into a spacious company flat with a large garden, complete with greenhouse, and in no time at all we were part and parcel of small town life. Llangollen is world famous as the home of the International Musical Festival, better known as the Llangollen *Eisteddfod*. The concept of uniting nations in a festival of song and dance was the brainchild of a handful of men, fired by the wish to demolish the barriers of colour, race and creed, and to bring people of the world together in harmonious competition following a divisive world war. Whilst we lived in 'Llan', my family vanished for the whole of *eisteddfod* week. Glen became involved in the floral committee and the children either sold programmes, or acted as stewards. I took very little part in the proceedings, primarily because I was left to supervise the skeleton staff that was maintained at the seed factory. The success of the event is due entirely to the people of Llangollen and district who still give their time willingly, voluntarily and with unbounded enthusiasm and to the untiring efforts of a highly efficient Secretary and Musical Director – the *eisteddfod*'s only two paid officials. It is proof positive of what can be achieved by a nucleus of dedicated thinkers and innovators, activated by a dream of peace and goodwill between nations.

Life in a small town can be hectic, though, as I soon discovered. Before I knew it, I was chairman of the local branch of the RSPCA and a member of the British Legion, the *Eisteddfod* Finance Committee, the Twenty Club and, as if that wasn't enough, a lay reader in church. The last was the result of a cry for help from the vicar, who held responsibility for four churches and for much of the time only himself and one other lay reader to conduct services. I felt ill-equipped in my role, but I'm told that my sermons were original if nothing else, especially the one in which I drew an analogy between the Trinity and 3-In-One lubricating oil.

The Twenty Club was a dramatic society, and for the first time since I had left school I found myself treading the boards again. We were fortunate in having several experienced producers, set designers, backstage helpers and excellent amateur actors among our members. We staged ambitious productions, including *The Crucible* in which I took the leading role of John Proctor. The play and the part affected me deeply, as the real life tale of cruel and bigoted inhabitants of the small town Salem in America emerged from Arthur Miller's brilliant portrayal. My experience of amateur acting was to prove of immense value later in life. I owe a lot to one producer in particular, who improved my diction, instilled stagecraft into my very amateur early efforts and rekindled my confidence in front of an audience.

In those days Llangollen boasted several characters and a number of them gathered nightly in the Jenny Jones tavern, to sup pints of good ale and exchange gossip and reminiscences. The pub was a free house run by the elder brother of seven sons, all of whom had served in the RAF during the war – surely a record. The public bar was so small and narrow that when its complement of about fifteen regulars was present there was just enough room to lift a foaming tankard to one's lips. The décor was a rich, warm brown, the result of decades of nicotine deposits. The walls hadn't had a lick of paint in living memory and we suspected that it was only the thick veneer of nicotine that prevented their collapse. Directly opposite the bar and no more than three feet from it a long well-worn bench ran the length of the wall. Every night it was occupied by five ancients, each with fascinating tales to tell of Llangollen in bygone days. I once calculated that their combined ages totalled nearly four hundred years, and I couldn't help but conclude that quaffing ale prolongs life! I spent many happy hours in their company and how I wish I'd had a tape recorder to log their stories.

One of Llangollen's real characters was the irrepressible 'Boyo' Hughes, who owned two shops in the main street – a newsagent's and a jeweller's. Soon after our arrival in Llan I had occasion to call at the newsagent's in search of a new pipe. The shop appeared to be empty, but I could hear faint 'noises-off' somewhere in the rear. I waited a few minutes, then shouted, 'Shop!' Boyo emerged, holding a shaving brush in one hand and a cut-throat razor in the other, with half his acquiline features covered in lather. I voiced my wish, he produced a tray of briars from under the counter and finished shaving while I made my choice and paid. Our second transaction, some months later, was equally bizarre. I wanted an alarm clock, called at the jeweller's and there was Boyo behind the counter. On request he produced three clocks, placed them on the glass counter and invited me to take my pick. Before I could do so, both he and I were enveloped in a cloud of steam issuing from a kettle somewhere in the vicinity of his feet. He ignored it completely. The swirling vapour was as thick as a morning mist on Dartmoor, but by touch and speech we made a deal and the clock I chose did sterling service for many years.

The British Legion Annual Dinner was a great event, attended by ex-servicemen from both wars. One of the veterans of the 1914–1918 conflict was both a neighbour and a great friend of mine. We were both Cardigan born and bred and these strong ties bridged the age gap as though it didn't exist. George was a brilliant after-dinner speaker and an

142

accomplished beer-drinker, and by the time festivities drew to a close his faculties were distinctly impaired. He lived about half a mile out of town and managed the erratic journey home by progressing in short, weaving bursts from one telegraph pole to the next. When he got to a pole he grasped it by both arms, focused on the next, got his bearings and set off again. In all the years I knew him, George never failed to make home port.

Then there was Edwards the butcher – a square peg in a round hole, if ever there was one. He was a gifted musician, compelled by his father to follow in the flesh-purveying business. Father was a devout, puritanical Methodist, and the whole of Sunday was devoted to worship in true Welsh non-conformist tradition. It is common knowledge that the Welsh lamb from the heather-grazed mountains is the tastiest, sweetest meat in all the world and pre-war the Edwards family did a roaring mail-order trade in the best cuts. The joints were cut, packed in sacking, labelled, trundled to the post office in a handcart and despatched to standing-order customers in London and elsewhere, every Monday by the first post. Picture, if you will, the teetotal Edwards family on a Sunday evening in the spring lamb season. They had returned from the chapel service, eaten their evening meal and now, father, mother and their two sons sit by the fire doing nothing, waiting. Down in the shop rows of dead lambs are waiting to be dismembered and packed, and wait they must, until the witching hour. In the Edwards' household the grandfather clock strikes twelve and as the last stroke fades, the family rise and hasten to the shop. Sacrosanct Sunday is over, they can now work, and this they do through the night and, as dawn breaks, neat packs of lamb are ready for the mail train. The eldest son was rather irreverent and a bit of a wag. The large shop had two doors, one at either end, and during the war a queue would form at one of them. Meat was rationed and the first come were served with the best cuts. This eldest son used to wait until a queue had formed at one of the doors, then he'd open the other and bawl, 'Methodists and sinners, stay where you are, everybody else up here!'

In the fifties and sixties Llangollen and all Wales was still 'dry' on Sunday. All the pubs were closed and a packed bus left the town and crossed the border into England where ale and spirits flowed freely, seven days a week. It returned after 'stop-tap' and disgorged an inebriated, happy crowd, among them a local chemist whose alcohol blood-level had to be maintained at all costs. A casual observer could be forgiven for thinking that the man was a keen golfer, as he was often seen carrying a golfing umbrella. In fact the gamp never saw a golf course, nor was it used to deflect raindrops. It was a repository for a couple of bottles of brown ale, for use in an emergency. He and I enjoyed many a pint together and I always knew when he was full to capacity – his head sagged slowly to the bar counter and he ceased to take an interest in current affairs.

The flat we occupied in Llangollen was about a mile out of town and, as I walked to and from the seed factory, I passed a highly desirable, detached house occupied by a retired Major and his wife, both in their eighties. Despite failing eyesight, he was a keen gardener, and when I passed I frequently stopped and chatted with him, and answered his gardening queries. One morning the phone rang in my office – it was the Major. He told me that he and his wife had decided to sell up and move to a more convenient, self-contained flat and asked whether I would like to buy the house. I replied that I would, very much, but that I doubted whether I had sufficient funds to meet its price on the open market. He told me that he would like me to have it, as he could then be confident that the garden would be in safe and caring hands. He suggested that I have the house valued by an independent valuer and that he would sell at the valuation figure. Nothing could be fairer than that, and so for the sum of £3,200 I bought a detached, three-bed-roomed house, garage, large greenhouse and a third of an acre, fully-stocked garden. Although the Major was 'well-heeled', he was his own DIY man and, although the house was in first-class condition, there were visible signs of his impaired-vision handiwork. Some of the electrical installation was hazardous, to put it mildly. Whenever he needed an extra light or power point, he had plugged in to an existing power point and run cables along skirting boards, over doors and along picture rails. There were wires everywhere, and it is a wonder that he and his wife hadn't been electrocuted! He had also painted the interior himself, doing the windows without removing the curtains, with the result that they were stuck to the woodwork. Still, at £3,200 I wasn't complaining!

Kim the corgi was still with us and lucky to be alive. He was born in Aberystwyth from Queenie, his mother, who died of heart failure the day after he was born. Queenie was Glen's dog and her cardiac weakness was known to us. We kept her indoors and under close supervision outdoors when she was in season, but a local Lothario worked a flanker on us. He got in through a half-open window when we were all out and Queenie succumbed to his advances. We knew that he was the father, because he was seen making his escape with a self-satisfied smirk on his face. Kim was born prematurely and with difficulty and was little bigger than a mouse. We sought the help of a vet who took one look at the little runt and pronounced that, without his mother, he was doomed. Glen refused to accept his verdict and after much cajoling he suggested feeding the pup with Cow & Gate powdered milk at a 50 per cent dilution, from a bottle fitted with a small teat as used to feed premature babies. He also stressed that the pup had to be kept at the level of warmth he would have enjoyed cuddled up to his mother.

We followed the vet's advice, fed him, kept him in a basket by the fire by day, and at night took him to bed with us in one of my socks, with just his head protruding. Kim accepted our ministrations without question, grew and lived with us for eleven years, but remained a half-sized corgi. His incongruous upbringing proved beyond doubt that environmental factors play just as important a role in animal (humans included) development, as do genetic, hereditary influences. Not having

145

known his mother, he looked on Glen and I as his parents. He was convinced that he was human, queued up with the children for his orange juice and cod liver oil, and attacked all dogs and other animals on sight.

Shortly after our move to Llangollen, Kim had acquired a playmate. As I passed through the reception area in the factory one day, I saw a cardboard box on the desk with a puppy's head peering over the top. The receptionist told me that the little waif was in need of a home, but no one had volunteered to provide it with one. 'It' was a she, a sleek-haired, black and tan, F^1-hybrid terrier. She looked at me with misty, appealing eyes and I fell in love with her there and then, and took her home. Kim hated her on sight, but such was her charm and cheek that he soon relented and allowed her to share his bed. We called her Kate and she was totally devoted to us for the fifteen years that we were privileged to know her. She accompanied us everywhere and our son Richard even took her hitch-hiking with him. When she died, a bit of us died with her.

In due course our two children reached adolescence, with all its attendant problems. Janice matured into a strikingly beautiful girl and a succession of hopeful young swains were soon beating a path to our door. One sought to curry favour by presenting me with a fresh Dee trout on each visit but, as Jan didn't fancy him, the supply soon dried up. She did well at school, attained the necessary O- and A-levels and left us to read botany at Aberystwyth, as I had done before her. In due course she graduated, simultaneously married a fellow student and within four months they left for Australia, where her new husband Peter joined an ICI research station. Their first baby girl, our first grandchild, was born in Melbourne, their second in Llangollen and their third in São Paulo in Brazil, where Peter was establishing a further research station. I couldn't help thinking how drastically life had changed in the space of one generation. I was born into a small, intimate Welsh community; a generation later my three grand-daughters are internationals and, before they were even

146

weaned, had traversed a world that, as a child, I knew only as locations on a school map.

As a teenager Richard became a rebel. Outside the home he championed every underdog in sight and often returned battle-scarred, but unbowed. In the home he eschewed logical discussion and became so fractious that his mother, in a fit of frustration, once threw a plateful of chips at him. He was so astonished that he walked out, collected an equally disenchanted friend and vanished. Glen was distraught with worry, but I wasn't. I knew that sooner or later our chick would return to the nest, to the love and security he had known from birth. Eventually, he contacted us from Leeds, where he and his pal were 'on the bins', and it wasn't long before despondency, deprivation and poor health brought our prodigal son back into the fold. We didn't kill the fatted calf; we didn't need to. Our son had 'come to his senses' and had come to terms with life's true values. He also did well at school, decided to enter the precarious acting profession and went off to train at the Rose Bruford School of Speech and Drama in Sidcup. He passed his exams and without any prompting from us went to the University of Kent at Canterbury, where he graduated in English and History. There he met his future wife, and he is now the proud father of a son and a daughter. Whatever I have achieved in life pales into insignificance compared with the joy and satisfaction of seeing our two children in happy, stable relationships and our five grandchildren hale and hearty and mentally equipped to fashion their own future. These are blessings beyond compare.

During the fifties, the Cuthbert Seed Company was expanding into a group of horticultural enterprises. Owned by Sir Clayton and Lady Russon, it had acquired many brand names, famed throughout the gardening fraternity. They included Bunyard's of Maidstone, Laxton's of Huntingdon, Fogwill's of Guildford and, more significantly, Dobies of Chester. The acquisition of Dobies gave the Company a very large share of the British Garden Seed industry. The general gardening public bought their seeds in pictorial packets over the counter and

Cuthberts had a 50 per cent share of that market, at least. The enthusiast bought his seeds through a mail-order catalogue, in which he could select his requirements from a wider range of over a thousand varieties of flower and vegetable seeds, and Dobies catered for his needs. When the garden seed industry was at its peak in the fifties and sixties, the Llangollen factory filled and despatched over fifty million packets of seeds annually. I saw them as fifty million promises of beauty and bounty, and I still regard seeds as mini-miracles. In those days, Dobies printed and posted three-quarters of a million catalogues every year. Most of them dropped through British letterboxes, but a fair number were mailed to customers the world over. Requests for a copy of the catalogue sometimes came from unexpected quarters. I still have a most unusual catalogue request that Dobies received in December 1965 from a potential customer in Okwagbe, wherever that is, and this is how it read:

'Dear Sir,
I am very happy to write you this letter. I want you to send me your free Catalogue of Seed book and when you send it to me I will very happy to see it. And I will make you a friend in my Country because you send me your free catalogue seed book and I will give you one of my daughters to marry. So I wish you to send it to me and I see that your Companies good one and may God help you and your handmaster of the companies.
Thank you your friend
Peter O. Mikoyo.

That was nearly forty years ago. I sent him a catalogue and I'm still waiting for the promised daughter to turn up!

In the early 1960s the nationally famous seed firm, Ryder's of St Albans, became yet another part of the Cuthbert group of companies. It was formed some time at the turn of the century by Sam Ryder, whose name will be forever on the lips of every golfer chasing a little white ball in the general direction of a hole in the ground. For it was he that initiated the now prestigious Ryder Cup competition. In the early 1960s Ryder's was struggling and ripe for a takeover. Sir Clayton seized the opportunity, bought the company, closed the premises in St Albans and moved the whole outfit to a building he owned in the village of Corwen, ten miles west of Llangollen. I was appointed to manage the new organisation and to turn loss into profit. The building we occupied was the old workhouse and one or two of my staff had actually been born there, due to the poverty of the twenties and thirties. I recall an elderly gentleman calling at the factory and telling me that he remembered attending Sunday School in the room I was using now as my office. He and many other children were too poorly-clad to qualify for admittance to the local churches and chapels. In those days the workhouse was the only, and inadequate, source of succour for the poor people of a village in an area dominated and mostly owned by two large estates who cared little, if at all, for their welfare. Even in the 1960s a lingering cloud of suppression seemed to hang over the place, heightened by the fact that the sun's rays disappeared behind Pen-y-Pigyn mountain from mid-November to mid-February.

Restoring Ryder's fortunes entailed spending long hours including weekends at my desk and, although home was only ten miles from my office, Glen and I decided to sell up and head west. We were again lucky. A cottage on the western boundary of one of the estates was for sale. It had a third of an acre of potential garden, the house was basically sound and the asking price in 1967 was £2,700. It stood on the south face of the mountain, a mile from Corwen, overlooking the Dee Valley with the Berwyn mountains as a backcloth. We bought it, moved in, repaired its faults and I set about creating a garden.

The third of an acre site presented a problem to someone like myself who enjoys growing and consuming a wide variety of fresh untainted vegetables and fruit. Most of the ground was at the front and at the gable end of the cottage, in full view of the lane that was the fairly busy back road that linked Corwen to the neighbouring village of Carrog. Glen flatly refused to allow our vegetables to be our shop window and me and my veg were relegated to a small piece of ground at the back of the cottage. Siting the greenhouse I needed was also controversial. I wanted to have it at the front and in the sun all day, but, as I already had one at the seed factory, Glen could not understand why we had to have another one. Finally, we compromised and I decided to erect a lean-to greenhouse on the east-facing wall of the house, out of sight and out of mind. The momentous decision was reached in November and led to the greatest clanger I've ever dropped in my gardening life. Given the all-clear, I was impatient and within minutes I was out with a tape measure. With the early morning winter sun on my face, I concluded that it wasn't a bad place to have a greenhouse. It would bask in the morning sun with welcome shade from midday to nightfall – but I had eyes, yet could not see. Standing smack in front of me was a massive sycamore, its canopy naked and unadorned, with the sun shimmering through its branches. The greenhouse came, it was erected and in the spring I filled it with tomato and pot plants. They grew and flourished, until the sycamore shot sap into its buds and burst into leaf. Deprived of sun, the greenhouse plants went into decline, developed every disease known to science and succumbed to heavy shade. I sold the greenhouse!

I then turned my attention to making an ornamental garden and, having created what became an attractive shrub and herbaceous border and two lawns, I decided on a couple of features to complete the picture. One gable end of the cottage faced due south, overlooking the valley where the River Dee flowed on its journey from Bala lake to the sea. Beyond rose the afforested Berwyn mountain range with the busy A5 at its feet, wending its tortuous way from London to Holyhead. It was the perfect place for a patio, in the eye of the sun and with a superb view of extensive countryside. All I needed was enough stone to build a retaining wall and to pave the patio. Once again, Lady Luck lent a hand. I discovered that a row of slate-stone cottages was in the process of being demolished in the village and, for a modest fiver, a local farmer agreed to deliver a trailer-load of the free and precious stones that are a joy to work with. Using a hammer and cold chisel, they split as cleanly and easily as slicing a loaf of bread. A five-feet-high wall went up in an many days and within a week the patio was ready to receive sunbathers, picnickers and anyone else seeking sun and solace.

The second feature was a failure. I decided to construct a garden pool, populated by beautiful aquatic plants and maybe a fish or two. The ground was heavy, stony clay. It sneered at a spade and succumbed only to a pickaxe and much sweat and swearing. Kim the corgi helped. He dug and scratched at one end while I laboured at the other. It was back-breaking work, but at last it was done and I filled it with water. Kim watched the water level rise and when he considered that the pool was deep enough, he dived in. He was deeply grateful that I'd built him a swimming-pool and took to taking daily dips. I resigned myself to having a plantless pool, but when one of our grand-daughters fell in, I filled it in and planted dahlias instead.

Our cottage nestled at the foot of Y Gaer – a Welsh word indicating that the mountain top had once been a stronghold where Celts had repelled invaders, and probably vice-versa, depending on which was the home team on the day. The two dogs and I climbed the path to the top, summer and winter, and from the summit on clear days I sat and gazed with awe at a vista that encompassed five counties, an unpolluted land-scape of farms, forests and peaceful villages set in a twentieth-century Shangri-la. The day's cares and woes fell away like autumn leaves in the solitude of a silence broken only by the sounds of the animals whose home it was. The Gaer was my 'balm of each day's life, sore labour's bath'.

The whole area teemed with wildlife. Glen was privileged to watch a stoat performing its dance of death, flashing its white underbelly in the sun as it mesmerised a blackbird into submission. She also had an unnerving experience when she came out of the front door one day to find out why some heifers were leaning on our front fence, and she was most annoyed to see one of them coming towards the house and trampling on the flowers lining the drive. She advanced, 'shoo-shooed' it and the beast turned and ambled back the way it had come. It was only when she closed the gate, and it turned and looked at her that she realised it was a bull. On another occasion we returned home around midnight and as I drove into the drive my headlights lit up a large boar, fast asleep by the hedge. I nudged him on to his feet, convinced him that he should leave and then phoned the police station. The constable who answered was not a bit surprised – he had discovered the animal wandering about and had escorted it into our drive, in the mistaken belief that it belonged to us.

It was all part and parcel of the joys of country living. In fact, there were animals all around us, with sheep the dominant species. There were thousands of them and, although I was not a farmer, I was unavoidably a very small cog in the sheep farming community. Sheep are enigmatic creatures. They are intelligent, at the same time idiotic, and they possess incredible endurance. Proof of a sheep's will to live came one morning during lambing time. The cottage looked out on a large field, separated from our garden by a pig wire fence. At around 7 a.m. one Monday morning, I was in the bathroom, shaving, and happened to glance out of the window to see a wee lamb hanging by one hind leg from the fence and on our side of it. I hurried through my ablutions, dressed, approached the lamb, gently released it from its self-imposed trap and carried it to the neighbouring farmer who, I knew, was its rightful owner. What he told me was amazing. He knew that one of his ewes had lambed some time on the Saturday, yet he could find no trace of her lamb. He had assumed it had fallen prey to a fox, shrugged his shoulders and accepted the inevitable. From our conversation, it became clear that the unfortunate lamb had been suspended, head down and by one leg for between twenty-four and thirty-six hours and had survived unharmed. According to the farmer, the newborn animal's incredible endurance was possible only because it had suckled its mother at least once since birth. As an illustration of a sheep's utter stupidity, I recall a day when, walking back from a trip up Y

152

Gaer and crossing an empty field, I noticed a movement in a hedge. It was a sheep, apparently stuck between the wire fence and the hawthorn hedge. Somehow I managed to get myself behind the animal, to find that all the witless creature need have done to free herself was back out, but stupidly, she kept trying to leave by the no-go route. It took several minutes of heaving at her hindquarters to extricate her and then she strolled off and began grazing as if nothing untoward had happened. The farmer had moved his flock two days prior to my tussle with the sheep's backside, so she must have endured forty-eight hours of privation – what an idiot, what a stoic.

Three more animal encounters are stored in my memorybanks. The first concerns a female blackbird and her brood. On one side of the vegetable garden a grass bank sloped up to a fence and a field beyond. To keep it nice and tidy, I sickled it two or three times a year and once, as the sickle sliced through the grass, it dislodged a nest holding four tiny blackbird chicks. I was aghast. I, who loved animals, had done this to a family that had entrusted itself to our garden and our guardianship. Hopefully, I picked up the undamaged nest, placed it back into its original position and restored the four chicks to their home. The nest had laid hidden and shaded from the sun until I had destroyed its natural camouflage; now it was fully exposed. To put things right, I built a low leafy shelter over the tiny tots and prayed that the mother had witnessed my efforts and would forgive my clumsiness. She did and continued to feed her chicks, even though I had to renew the camouflage regularly as the foliage wilted. I believe she knew that it had been an accident and that in my ham-fisted way I was trying to make amends. I am sure that animals know instinctively who their human friends are and who are their enemies. Our birds trusted us implicitly. A robin built a nest above our back door, and a shy thrush raised a family in a box hedge no more than ten feet from our front door. Even more surprisingly, a pair of chaffinch set up home in a 'Lasurstern' clematis right alongside the front door that was in constant use. We were privileged to have won their trust.

Birds were not the only animals that 'leased' parts of our house. In spring and summer we seldom used the sitting-room, preferring to spend our days and evenings with our animals in the large kitchen. We hadn't lit a fire in the sitting-room for several weeks, until Glen decreed that it needed an airing. I laid the fire, lit the paper and the room filled with smoke. Not a wisp went up the chimney and I concluded that there was a structural fault somewhere in the stack. I rang a local two-brothers builder's firm, and they came the same afternoon. They raised a ladder and the elder brother scaled it to the roof, armed with a stout length of wood. Clutching the chimney-pot with one hand, he poked the stick down the stack with the other and then it happened – a furious, furry body sprang out of the chimney-pot and went for the builder's throat. He clouted it. It fell to the roof, rolled down, dropped over twenty feet on to the hard stone patio, shook itself and a squirrel shot across the lawn and up an ash tree. Its cosy, leafy nest was removed, no damage was done and I lit a good fire.

We sold up and left our Corwen cottage in September 1979, but not before we had experienced another close encounter with an animal, which has influenced our lives very deeply ever since. On a February afternoon in that year we were sitting at our table by a window that overlooked the snow-covered drive. I had cleared a patch of snow and sprinkled a few breadcrumbs for the birds when they suddenly scattered and a painfully thin and weak black cat appeared and began licking up the crumbs. It was obviously starving, so Glen cut up some raw liver and I put it outside. The cat ran off when I opened the door, but as soon as I returned indoors, it came back, ate the lot and disappeared. The following morning I found it, fast asleep in a dry soil-bed hollow under the box hedge. In its exhausted condition and with a full stomach, it remained comatose for nearly two days. When it awoke, it came to the conclusion that it should stay with us. We never knew where the cat had come from, but it was apparent that it was wild. It refused to accept our invitations to join us indoors, so I constructed a cat-flap in the door of the coal house, put its plate of food just inside and a comfortable bed nearby. The food proved irresistible, the bed likewise and the cat was halfway to becoming part of the family. Kim just accepted it.

I've called the cat 'it' because it is very difficult to determine a cat's sex at close quarters, let alone at long distance. Was it a she or a he? The cat solved the problem for us. Within a month or so, it became apparent that it was pregnant and I promptly christened her 'Marigold'. I've no idea why, because she looked more like a pansy 'King of the Blacks' than a member of the genus *Tagetes*. In April, with veterinary assistance, she gave birth to two kittens, of which she was immensely proud. Thenceforth she joined us in the house, while still keeping us at arm's length unless she wanted something. Having started a horticultural nomenclature, I continued by naming the kittens 'Daisy' and 'Sweet William'. I got it half-right and half-wrong, because Sweet William turned out to be a female, but with, as our vet put it, 'an identity problem'. I think she's more of a transsexual than anything and is quite happy to be called William.

In the wild Marigold must have been sex-starved, because she soon fell in love with a big, good-natured, good-looking tabby who visited her regularly. Their love prospered and once again Marigold grew large and rotund 'with kitten'. We moved house towards the end of her pregnancy and the 130-mile journey from Corwen to near Chepstow proved harrowing for Glen. We packed Marigold into a cardboard cat-box and the two kittens into a wickerwork cat-basket, then loaded them all into Glen's Mini. I took Kim and a full load of bits and pieces in my Ford Escort Estate. We set off in convoy with the Mini following the Ford and, although the weather turned wet, we made excellent progress until we reached the outskirts of Ludlow. The Mini's headlights started flashing, so we pulled into the next lay-by and I went to make enquiries. It was pouring with rain, yet the car's window was wide open and as I stuck my head in, the reason became clear – there was a strong aroma of 'puss-poop'. Daisy had been 'taken short' and, as cats will not foul their own nests, she had somehow managed to squeeze out between the bars of her basket, and joined Glen in the front to make her 'deposit' there. We still had fifty miles to go and my wife, with a handkerchief over her nose, had to drive all the wet way with the rain beating in through her open window.

Within two weeks of our arrival in our new home Marigold begat again, this time two beautiful toms, one white-fronted, white-footed black and one gorgeously marked, tortoise-shell, more handsome even than his father. I called them 'Alyssum' and 'Chrysanthemum', or Aly and Chrys for short. We now had five cats, comprising two neutered females and two similarly deprived males, and our feline menage was deeply upsetting to the local ginger tom, Romeo, a devil incarnate. He very nearly bit the tails off Aly and Chrys and he cruelly raped Marigold, resulting in a third pregnancy. She gave birth to three kittens, one as black as night and the other a black-pawed tabby – the third died soon after birth. I christened the two survivors 'Cassiope' (Cass) and 'Bartonia' (Barty) respectively. At this time Marigold was in poor health. She had cat flu and passed the ailment on to her new-born kittens and left them to die. They were a pathetic pair, with noses so full of mucus they could hardly breathe. Glen, as ever, refused to be beaten and together we fed them evaporated milk and glucose through a syringe. The kittens fought with us every inch of the way and with the help of the local vet, they won through. Having endowed us with six cats, Marigold's health declined rapidly and within a short time of her last confinement, she was put to sleep peacefully.

While she was fit and well, Marigold was a superb mother. She devoted herself to the welfare of the four eldest, taught them to hunt and to be aware of life's perils. She even taught them the Green Cross Code and they never traverse the lane without first pausing and looking both ways. She was too feeble to train her last two offspring, so, to our astonishment, their two elder brothers each took one kitten under a wing and drilled them in the art of self-sufficiency and survival. The cats are now twelve years of age, and during our time together we have learnt to respect and wonder at their superhuman senses of sight, smell, hearing and communication. They understand our spoken word and they read our minds, a faculty that can be disconcerting at times. Among many instances of unspoken communication there is one that it still inexplicable. Some ten years ago, when Barty was still a youngster, we were sitting in the drawing-room, watching television in front of a roaring log fire. The night was pitch black and suddenly, without rhyme or reason, I rose, grabbed a torch and rushed outside. In the beam of the torch and some distance away I saw Barty, locked in the death-grip of the accursed ginger tom, whose razor-sharp claws had almost disembowelled him. I roared my rage, charged and the tom fled. Barty was badly lacerated, but thanks to our vet's expertise, he was stitched up and made a rapid and miraculous recovery. No less miraculous and mysterious was the silent SOS he had sent, seeking my aid.

We love our cats, they love us and Cass' recent death from cancer affected us all. We mourned his passing and for twelve days the other cats mourned with us. They ate very little and just lay around looking sad and dejected. They live as a family, yet each is fiercely individual and they have a pecking order and a code of behaviour that the human race would do well to emulate.

We spent that first week in our new home unpacking numerous boxes and tea-chests and organising ourselves. Our three cats resented the move and sulked for days, until it dawned on them that they were here to stay. The birth of the two kittens within a fortnight of our arrival kept Marigold busy, and young Daisy and William were so intrigued by the new arrivals that they forgot to be homesick. In the garden, my first priority was to feed the family, although now it was only two in number. I needed help, someone to clear the undergrowth at the back and, having cleared it, to rotovate it to a workable, plantable soil. I headed for the local tavern. Gathered there in front of frothy pints I found, as expected, a fount of knowledge, far superior to *Yellow Pages*. Pub regulars always know who does a good job at a fair price and I still go there in search of advice and a tankard of fine ale. A man armed with a sickle, flame-gun and rotovator duly arrived, saw to the soil and I planted the whole area (about a quarter of an acre) with potatoes, to clear the ground. In the virgin earth they grew like things possessed and for almost a year we ate them boiled, roasted, sautéed, croquetted, chipped, jacketed and crisped. Spuds were on the menu twice daily and I had them for breakfast as well, if there were any left from the previous day.

Now I grow just a couple of rows of 'earlies', for the indescribable pleasure of savouring the taste of new potatoes in June. The remainder of the vegetable garden is carefully planned to provide us with some fresh vegetables every week of the year. There is an inevitable summer glut and Glen is hard-pressed to keep pace with freezing the surplus for winter use. I confess that I take great pride and pleasure in bringing a trug basket brimming with harvest-fresh untainted vegetables to the kitchen. I feel as a caveman must have done when he brought home the kill, and I'm sure that my instinct to provide is a throwback to my youth, when we grew to survive. In those days the nearest greengrocer was seven miles away and handy packs of frozen vegetables were as unlikely as space travel.

Up on the bank I planted fruit trees and ornamental trees and bushes, and around and beneath them hundreds of daffodils and narcissi. Bill Sowerbutts, former 'Gardener's Question Time' panellist, was once asked to nominate his favourite flower and without a moment's hesitation he replied, 'Cauliflower'. When he ran a market garden he reckoned he made more money from growing and selling cauliflowers than from anything else. My first floral choice is the daffodil. Who can resist flowers with names like Unsurpassable, Golden Harvest, Fortune and Ice Follies? They are among the first flowers to despatch winter's gloom, with their spectacular golden trumpets heralding the advent of spring, and they love to be left alone to grow and multiply in grass. I had to plant the bank with due consideration to Mother Nature who had beaten me to it. Now in spring there are carpets of bluebells, wood anemones, clumps of primroses and cowslips and little groups of sweet-scented violets. Later in the season the bank tends to 'go wild', but in among the long grass peep columbines and campion, scabious and speedwell, herb-Robert and bugle, scarlet pimpernel and cow parsley, wood sorrel and dandelions, St John's wort and more. I wait for them to finish flowering and seeding and call in a strimming neighbour to tidy things up.

By now there are several ornamental trees on the bank, chosen either for their flowers, their foliage or their berries, but the first two to go in were our respective favourites. To keep Glen happy, I planted a Mountain Ash which, she claims, keeps witches at bay and – Do you know what? – she's right! We haven't seen a single witch since I planted it! My special tree is *Koelreuteria paniculata*, more easily remembered and pronounced as the Golden Rain Tree, or Pride of India. Long ago I fell for its pinky-green, fern-like foliage in spring, its autumn bronze and, in between times, the great gush of summer gold as its flower panicles thrust upwards from the tips of the topmost branches. It has only flowered once in seven years, because it is a touch tender, but the good things in life are worth waiting for and I have a gardener's patience. And so the garden is taking shape, but it is far from finished. Is a garden ever finished? Is a gardener ever satisfied? No, we plant this and that, then we move them to what we believe is a better place, but it isn't and so we move them again. My mother spent half her lifetime seeking in vain for the best place to grow rhubarb. She moved the poor thing every year, which so upset it that we seldom enjoyed its juicy sticks.

To get back to seeds, the Ryder business was perking up nicely when Sir Clayton made what I believe was a fatal mistake – he bought the renowned seed firm, Carter's of Raynes Park, holders of the Royal Warrant, which he greatly coveted. All the Board's attention and reserves were diverted to resighting the entire Carter operation in Llangollen. Ryder's was axed, the hard-working, loyal staff were made redundant and I returned to Llangollen.

Then, without warning, Sir Clayton suffered a fatal heart attack. Lady Russon was devastated by her husband's sudden and untimely demise and had little option but to look for a buyer for the company that she and Sir Clayton had lovingly built up over a period of about forty years. The net result was that we acquired a new chairman with a proven success record in marketing and promoting nationally known food brands. Unfortunately, he was ignorant of the intricacies and peculiarities of the seed industry, marketing, merchandising and selling techniques. We suddenly found ourselves top-heavy with promotional executives – so called whiz-kids, with about as much whiz as a damp squib. In short, the company had almost more shepherds than sheep, and a sheepdog that had little idea how to drive them to greener pastures. In the space of a decade a catalogue of mismanagement and a lust for power had all but destroyed a company name that had held the respect and admiration of the gardening world for well over a century. For me it was an end and a new beginning.

A New Beginning

ℒ

MOST of my life has been determined by chance, by just being in the right place at the right time, and my involvement in the media was no exception. In Llangollen we lived a few doors away from David John and his family. He was the Agricultural Advisor for the county, but in 1960 they sold up and left. It transpired that he had applied for the post of Agricultural Producer for BBC Wales in Cardiff and had been appointed. It was at the time when gardening programmes on radio and television were gaining popularity and David was asked to initiate a fifteen-minute Welsh-language gardening programme for Welsh radio listeners. He needed someone who knew a lot about gardening and who was a fluent Welsh speaker, and I was the only one he could think of who qualified on all counts,

So, in June 1960 a new direction to my professional life began, when I made by first gardening broadcast in Welsh. In the early days of the programme all our broadcasts were live, and I sat alone in the BBC Bangor studio every Friday evening, and for fifteen minutes told my Welsh-speaking listeners what they could and should be doing in their gardens. So it continued for a year or so, until the producer decided to emulate Radio 4's 'Gardeners' Question Time' and I became one of three panellists, with a chairman to maintain a semblance of order. He and I occupied the Bangor studio with a radio link to my co-panellists in Cardiff. We proffered topical gardening tips and answered listeners who had written to us about their gardening problems. For several years I made the weekly round trip from Llangollen to Bangor along the A5 through some of the most beautiful countryside in Britain. In summer the wooded valley of Betws-y-Coed teemed with visitors and the crags around Capel Curig and Nant Francon Pass were dotted with climbers. Even Ogwen Lake looked calm and inviting. In autumn the trees were gorgeously resplendent in their foliar finery, but with the coming of winter the scene changed. The sightseers stayed beside their warm suburban hearths, only a few hardy climbers still braved the elements and the journey to and from Bangor had to be negotiated with extreme care. The waters of Ogwen were black, disturbed and threatening. The peaks were under deep snow, and the road was frequently icy and white with snow, but I never failed to make it to the studio and back. The chairman and I had a standing arrangement – we met for half an hour or so before the broadcast in the bar of The Belle View, where we lubricated our tonsils with a 'medicinal' beverage, dispensed by Miss Hughes and her bachelor brother. The beer was good, the place was spotless and over the fireplace hung a large framed parchment, bearing the signatures of broadcasters whose names are history. They included Tommy Handley and Jack Train of ITMA (*'It's That Man Again'*) fame – the comedy radio programme that raised a laugh in every wartime household with a wireless set. The entire BBC Light Entertainment Unit had been evacuated from London to Bangor to escape the bombing, and its artists were essential to the war effort; they maintained morale at a time when the British public heard little but bad news of defeat and withdrawal. They too sought solace in The Belle View and in the warm welcome of its friendly innkeepers.

With a tentative and very amateur foot in the BBC door, I decided to widen my horizons and try my hand at writing gardening articles. I approached the editor of the *Wrexham Leader* and he very kindly agreed to accept a weekly article on a trial basis. They passed muster and my weekly gardening column appeared in the paper for several years, until I felt that it was time to give it a rest. I'm still grateful to the *Leader* and its editor for the opportunity it gave me to launch myself into the literary world of gardening. Without it, I wouldn't be writing this book. The acceptance and success of the articles in the local paper fired me with enthusiasm. I even bought a new pen! Since those early days I have written for most of the gardening press and many other publications, and presently my horticultural ramblings appear weekly in *The Lady* magazine – a publication that has appeared on newsagents' shelves for over a hundred years. I have also written four gardening books. Some day I might write another, when the writer's cramp I've contracted writing this one is cured!

Following my regular weekly contributions to the '*Garddio*' programme, my voice and I were becoming familiar to Welsh-speaking listeners and BBC Cymru gave me a further opportunity to spread my wings. I was invited to make a weekly gardening advice slot on an early morning magazine programme, called 'Helo *Bobol*' ('Hello Everyone'). This meant leaving home at 6 a.m. for an unmanned studio in Wrexham to be on air live for five or six minutes at about 7.15 a.m. An unmanned studio is the loneliest place on this planet. It is totally soundproof, there are no technicians and at the press of a master switch everything is activated. In theory, and usually in practice, a disembodied voice in one's earphones issues instructions. It doesn't always happen. On my first assignment I found the studio locked. I phoned the BBC in Cardiff, who had forgotten to inform the 'keeper of the key' that I was scheduled to make an historic broadcast to the Welsh nation for five whole minutes! The 'key' figure arrived and let me in just in time to make my contribution. When I had finished, the disembodied voice told me that it, or they, would send me my own door key, which they did. It was the wrong one and the key-man was called to the rescue yet again. On another occasion I let myself into the building, saw that the on air, red light was on above the studio and waited in the ante-room-cum-toilet. Finally, the red light went out, the door opened and a fellow who used the studio every day to present a local news report, emerged. We passed a few pleasantries, he departed and I went into the studio and said my piece. I felt the usual sense of relief that it had gone without a hitch, until I found that the studio door was locked from the outside and my key wouldn't unlock it from the inside. For a few minutes I panicked. Even if I yelled my head off, no one would hear me in my soundproof tomb. I had visions of being found years later, a sweater-clad skeleton seated, sightless, in front of an equally dead microphone, petrified for ever in the dry, deoxygenated air of the sealed sarcophagus. My mind ran riot. I saw myself as the Tutankhamun of Wales, mummified to posterity with the rusted trappings of the twentieth century the only clue to my identity. My panic subsided, as I realised that Glen knew where I was and I noticed a telephone on a chair by the table. I couldn't recall the BBC telephone number, so I rang home, Glen rang Cardiff, they rang the man with the key and he came and released me from my prison.

It is with considerable pride that I can claim never to have failed to turn up for a broadcast in thirty-two years of speaking into an inanimate chunk of metal called a microphone. The odd thing is that the moment I open my mouth the mike disappears and in its place I sense an audience. I feel a strange, intimate relationship with people in their homes, their cars and their workplaces who have switched on and are listening to me. Even in the confines of a small cubicle that passes for an unmanned studio, I am transported into a listening world that encompasses the whole of Britain and beyond.

Despite my many years on air there have been very few occasions when things didn't go according to plan. The nearest I came to missing a programme occurred many years ago, while I was still the sole contributor to 'Garddio'. The programme went out live every Friday evening at 7.15 p.m. and I was usually in the Bangor studio well before time. On this occasion I had spent the week in St Albans on company business and had arranged with my producer that I would drive to BBC Swansea to do the broadcast. My transport was a Ford transit van that was the company's property. It had been agreed that I would collect it from the company's subsidiary firm at St Albans and drive it to Llangollen via Swansea. I set off in good time, with the assurance that the van had recently been serviced and was in tip-top condition. In those days the M4 wasn't even a pile of rubble and my east-to-west journey took me along busy A-class roads. All went well for many miles, until the cab temperature became tropical and it filled with ominous blue smoke. I stopped at a small garage in a village and explained my predicament to the sympathetic owner. He lifted the bonnet, peered into an abyss of blue haze, got a wet rag and very gingerly unscrewed the radiator cap. The water in the radiator was obviously at boiling point and, with the last twist, the cap shot up into the air, described a graceful arc and fell into a duck pond alongside the garage. We looked at each other. Then the garage owner and I removed our shoes and socks and rolled our trousers up above the knees. His daughter went one better. She took off her tight-fitting trousers and, in her knickers, joined her father and I in the duck pond. The search took almost an hour and by the time we found it the engine of the van had cooled sufficiently to allow for the opening of the drainage tap. Out oozed a liquid the colour and consistency of hot chocolate. We filled the radiator with clean water. I topped up with petrol, paid, thanked my good samaritans and drove off. I had lost valuable time and knew that there wasn't a minute to spare if I was to reach Swansea in time. I put my foot down and, within the limits imposed by the traffic heading west, broke all speed regulations. I was within ten miles or so of my destination when, to my horror, the cab again filled with blue smoke. I opened the window and drove on – I had to, even when a jet of brown liquid hit the windscreen. I put the wipers to work and a few minutes later pulled up outside the BBC in a blue cloud. The producer was waiting. We raced up the stairs and entered the studio just as the sports reporter vacated his chair. I slid into it, my producer sat opposite, the red light came on, we were live on air and the producer said, 'Well, Clay, what should we be doing in the garden this weekend?' (in Welsh) – Oh calamity! In the rush I'd left my script in the van, so I ad libbed my way through and when I'd finished, the producer said, 'That was great.' I haven't used a script since. Later, as he and I relaxed over a pint, I asked him what he would have done if I'd failed to appear. 'Well,' he said, 'I was going to put a record on – "In A Monastery Garden".'

Considering my 29 years on the 'Garddio' programme, there were surprisingly few mishaps. Once, we were scheduled to record our programme in a small village in North Wales and, on arrival at the village hall, we found that the whole area was blacked-out by a power cut. Someone produced three paraffin-fuelled, hurricane lamps for our team and the BBC van used its own power to record the programme. The hall was in darkness and that was the only time that we completed a recording in front of an invisible audience. There was another infamous evening when we completely failed to fulfil our function, but that wasn't our fault. We arrived at a village school in good time, our audience trickled in and I'm sure we would have recorded an epic programme if only the BBC recording van had turned up! It was somewhere else recording a religious programme.

When I first began broadcasting in 1960, 'Garddio' was a weekly programme with a large and appreciative audience. Sadly, it is now transmitted on a three-weekly basis, which reflects the decline in the Welsh-speaking population. I am neither a Welsh Nationalist, nor have I set fire to any holiday cottages, but it is my fervent hope that the language will live, for if it dies, its culture will die with it. I was once told that Welsh is now the oldest spoken language in the world and my informant was an Indian Sanskrit scholar, whom I chanced upon in a transit camp near Calcutta in 1946. He recognised my accent and asked me to utter a few sentences in Welsh. We compared notes and I was amazed at the many similarities between my mother tongue and the Far Eastern written, unspoken, Sanskrit. He may have been wrong, but he sounded convincing.

In 1962 we were still living in Llangollen. I was a regular panellist on 'Garddio' and making spasmodic, by-invitation contributions to the long defunct radio programme 'In Your Garden', chaired by the late Roy Hay. I was content with my lot and had no further media ambitions, but the media had other ideas. In December of that year I had a phone call from BBC Television Birmingham, inviting me to make a guest appearance on 'BBC Gardening Club', an immensely popular programme hosted by the incomparable Percy Thrower. It was a free and easy pre-Christmas chat programme and my fellow guests were Professor Alan Gemell, Roy Hay, and Percy's father-in-law, who had retired from the post of head gardener at Windsor. I was so nervous that I can remember little, but I recall that we were asked, 'What do you dislike most about gardening, or gardeners?' My reply was: 'Gardeners who invite you to look at their gardens and then tell you that you should have come last week when so and so was in bloom, or next week when such and such a plant will be at its beautiful best.' My television debut passed the test and I was invited back the following week and subsequently I made several appearances a year on 'Percy's Programme'.

Thirty years ago television gardening was very different from today's sophisticated and colourful productions. Our programmes were recorded in a large studio in Gosta Green in Birmingham and they were in black and white, which meant we had to remember to describe every flower. Our garden was a heap of soil on the studio floor, held in place by old railway sleepers. We sowed and planted everything in it, including trees, and when the recording was over we heaved them out again. There was also a small greenhouse without glass, in which I once made a thoughtless mistake. I was inside it, Percy was outside and without thinking I passed him a tray of seedlings through the 'glass'. Not everyone can do that!

In the mid to late sixties it all changed. We began filming in colour and I had the privilege of co-presenting the BBC's first gardening programme in glorious technicolour. The colour was good, but it wasn't perfect. Everything white had a thin red edge to it and things like dark blue lobelias tended to look mauvey-purple. But, best of all, we forsook the studio and ventured outdoors into real gardens, on real soil and where greenhouses had glass panes and when it rained we got wet. 'BBC Gardening Club' became 'Gardeners' World' which, for several years, was recorded at Clack's Farm near Worcester, before moving on to its present location at Barnsdale in Rutland. I moved with it and gradually assumed the role of interviewer as the programme travelled all over Britain, visiting large and small private gardens.

I was in my true element with people and plants. My interviewees came from all walks of life, from allotment holders to owners of stately homes. The common denominator was their love of plants and their plots of ground, which they readily shared with me and the many million viewers who followed our programmes. I enjoyed their company and their conversation, and learnt more about plants than I dreamt there was to learn. I also realised how little I knew of a subject so vast. Only a fraction can be learnt in one lifetime, but it's great fun learning.

Compared to radio, television work is much more demanding and time consuming. Recording a half-hour radio programme will not take up more than an hour of an experienced broadcaster's time at most and, if it's live, it is completed within its allotted time. In contrast, recording a thirty-minute television gardening programme often takes two days, which includes the time taken to plan it on site beforehand. I confess that I frequently got fed up to the teeth, waiting for the camera to be in position, for the sun to shine, for the rain to stop, for the producer to return from the toilet or whatever. I didn't mind hanging about in the summer warmth, but in winter the cold could penetrate right through layers of clothing to the very marrow. The coldest I've ever felt was on a catwalk between some yachts in the marina at Falmouth. The garden we were recording stood at the very top of a cliff, overlooking the marina, and our imaginative producer decided to open the programme with the camera trained on the garden from below. An icy, easterly wind whistled down the River Fal and the microphone pinned to my chest refused to function properly.

Despite the sound engineer's ministrations, it emitted a loud, crackling noise. He tried everything, including shoving the ice-cold mike down inside my trousers and strapping it to my inside leg. It was agony. By the time we got the thing to work, I was so cold, that someone had to hold the mug of hot tomato soup which a sympathetic soul had made for me.

The weather could be kind, it could be cruel; we could be lucky, or unlucky. Luck was definitely on our side when we went to record a 'prog' at Lanhydrock garden in Cornwall. We previewed the garden in the morning of a sky-blue early May day. The place is renowned for its majestic magnolias and on that clear day they were in full, breathtaking bloom, their large chalices gazing open-mouthed into the sun. Over lunch I suggested to the producer that we should film them that afternoon, having in mind that I could head for home early on the following day. He agreed and we shot a few minutes of wonderful film. We stayed at a local hotel and when I drew the curtains in the morning I looked out on a landscape white with hoar frost. We had breakfast, returned to Lanhydrock and found every single magnolia petal on the ground, wrenched from its high perch by the fingers of frost. We have cheated sometimes – I have actually stuck a petal or two back on a plant when they've dropped off before we'd finished filming, but there was no way anyone could stick several thousand *Magnolia campbellii* petals back on their branches, fifty feet up in the air.

'You can't win them all,' as the saying goes, and on one occasion at Barnsdale we very nearly lost all! We filmed the first half of the programme on a Tuesday and on Wednesday returned to find the garden under an inch of snow. If we had continued filming, the viewer would have seen a garden suddenly transformed from brown earth and green grass to a carpet of white in the bat of an eyelid and not even a television producer could explain that. So we all went home, the snow melted, and we returned to complete the filming on the Friday. The programme was scheduled for transmission that evening at 8.30 p.m. and from noon onwards we had a despatch rider standing by, ready to whisk the finished article from Barnsdale to Pebble Mill in Birmingham. We made it, but it was a close thing.

Having taken part in hundreds of television gardening programmes, some were forgettable, most were memorable and a few were unique experiences. The most magical and mysterious happened at the magnificent Bodnant Gardens in North Wales. The plan of action had been determined beforehand and on the day of filming the producer decided to open the programme in the very early morning. I was to be found, standing in the cradle of the Dell, with the camera perched high on a spur near the top terrace looking down on the scene below. It was one of those mornings when fairy tales can come true. The new-born sun cast shafts of golden beams through the haze-shrouded trees and below my feet a stream murmured its music. There wasn't a civilised sound as I stood on a wooden bridge, almost expecting to see the little people, but they never came. A shout from on high brought me back to reality. I said my piece, got the thumbs-up signal and was left with my thoughts. I lit my pipe and lingered a while, reluctant to break the magical spell of the peaceful place, but there was work to be done and I soon started up the wooded path. At the top the trees opened on to grassland with a small copse in the middle and, as I emerged, I saw a white-suited lady carrying a coat over her arm, walking across the grass until she passed out of sight behind the copse. I thought she was Jean, the producer's assistant, and waited for her to reappear at the other end of the copse, but she didn't. I crossed over, searched high and low, but saw no sign of her and it transpired that Jean hadn't been anywhere near there. I've often wondered who my white lady was and how she had happened to cross into my time span, or I into hers. I shall never know.

My visits to gardeners and their gardens all over Britain brought me face to face with both beauty and reality. Time and again I have met gardeners whose disabilities would have condemned lesser mortals to despair and even death. For these people their love of plants and their cultivation transcends their sickness, and they are among the most cheerful people I've ever met. They confirmed my own conviction that gardening is mentally and physically therapeutic and that in one's own garden lies the means of escape from life's trials and tribulations. My garden is my bolt-hole. I frequently return home on a summer's evening dead tired, having driven long distances on traffic-snarled roads. I shed my glad-rags, don my gardening gear and by the time I've done an hour's work I'm fully relaxed and my weariness has disappeared. I'm fortunate to have an acre of ground to satisfy my compulsion to grow things, whereas some enthusiasts must make do with far less. A very determined lady I know tends a balcony garden 200-feet up at the very top of a tower block in the London area where, believe it or not, it rains upwards when the wind blows. We recorded a television programme in her unlikely garden with the cameraman roped to a concrete pillar, and I still wonder at the lady's determination to grow flowers and vegetables against such long odds.

Yet there are times when I wonder whether some gardeners take their hobby too seriously. I remember the Geordie pot-leek fanatic who grew hundreds of the things and nothing else. They demanded his undivided attention for fifty weeks of the year, leaving just two weeks in November when he took himself and his wife off on holiday. When I interviewed him, he was the world champion pot-leeker and his terraced house was furnished with the prizes his leeks had earned for him. As he told me himself, he liked nothing better than to have 'a good leek in the garden'! In the same north-eastern corner of England I met a vegetable show winner with his own special brand of liquid fertiliser. Outside his greenhouse stood a massive metal canister full to the brim with a dark, evil-smelling liquid. His recipe included doses of blood from a nearby abattoir, a sack of cow manure, which was suspended in the canister, and numerous other secret ingredients. all topped with two bottles of Newcastle Brown Ale. Any one of his cabbages would have fed a family of ten and his carrots were a yard long. He himself was the picture of health, and I still wonder whether he drank the malodorous magic potion himself.

To pursue and enjoy his hobby, a gardener needs to be philosophical and he must have endless patience. I have grown accustomed to the loss of cherished plants due to the vagaries of the weather, or to the attention of unexpected pests and diseases. When it happens, my fellows and I shrug our shoulders, blame no one and begin all over again – *c'est la guerre*. Nature commands patience. She cannot be hurried. There is a time to sow, a time to grow, a season for all things and woe betide the gardener who foolishly tries to beat the clock. Patience is indeed a virtue, instilled into me at an early age by the placid behaviour of plants and projected into my everyday life to considerable advantage. One of the most patient gardeners I ever knew was besotted with begonias. At the time, I was presenting a Welsh television programme, called *'Dewch I'r Ardd'* ('Come Into The Garden'), and we paid regular visits to his garden during spring and summer. He grew over eight thousand large-flowered begonias from seed and, as most gardeners know, begonia seedlings are smaller than small. He spent hours bent over his seed trays, pricking out the pygmy plants and that, I maintain, spells patience with a capital P.

Some years ago the BBC made a valiant attempt to present gardening as a fun pursuit. I was invited to present a television programme called 'Dig This', which was informative, with the hard facts proffered with humour. A programme dealing with the planting of a bottle garden involved a young actress and I dressed in white lab coats, in the roles of nurse and doctor respectively. We boarded a hatchback car with a stretcher in the rear and I drove at breakneck speed down a dual carriageway under police supervision to a tower block in Birmingham suburbia. My instructions were explicit – 'When you leave the carriageway, screech round the corner and you will see a cameraman lying in the road facing you. Skid to a halt a few feet from him, dash out of the car, grab the stretcher and run with the nurse to a concrete little-bin where you will find an empty discarded carboy. Remove it, place it on the stretcher, run to the tower block and take the lift to the roof.' There we found a table, complete with plants, compost and all the accoutrements necessary for planting a bottle garden and, in the corner, a tent into which the nurse disappeared. I planted the bottle garden in a young gale and when I'd finished, my partner emerged from the tent bearing a bottle of champagne and two glasses and we toasted something – probably the fact that I hadn't killed the courageous cameraman lying in the road!

On the celebration of Halloween the producer's imagination ran riot. We had hollowed-out, candle-lit, evil-faced pumpkins, and I was kitted out as an evil warlock in my gardening boots, black stocking tights, starched shirt, winged collar, bowtie, top hat and a long black cloak, and I flew over Birmingham on a broomstick. Yes, I did! And this is how it was done: they sat me astride a child's swing, with a broom between my legs and with the seat and the supporting ropes painted a light blue. For reasons beyond my understanding, the blue bits were invisible to the camera, and to all intents and purposes I glided over an area of the city – depicted on a large blown-up picture to my rear. To add an authentic touch to my flight of fancy, a wind machine blew a strong gust in my face, making my cloak float out behind me in the turbulent air. It was all great fun and I was sorry when the series was axed for reasons of economy.

In May 1976 my phone rang and I recognised the caller's voice before he introduced himself. He was Ken Ford, the producer of Radio 4's 'Gardeners' Question Time' and he invited me to join the panel of gardening gurus on a programme to be recorded in Liverpool in July. I had been a regular listener and ardent admirer of 'GQT' for many years and, without hesitation, leapt at the chance. I felt truly privileged to be asked to join a team of panellists who, in 1976, had been together on radio for almost thirty years – surely a record that will never be surpassed. In those days the regulars were Fred Loads, Bill Sowerbutts and Professor Alan Gemell and, to put it bluntly, they were 'knocking on a bit'. Ken, who also chaired the programme in the wake of Freddie Grisewood and

Franklin Engleman, was a very astute fellow. He realised that he needed a few first reserves to fill in, if and when a regular fell ill or decided to retire. I was one of many on trial and I passed the test.

To take part in my first 'GQT', I was instructed to make my way to the Bessie Braddock Hall on the outskirts of Liverpool. I couldn't find the place. Like the proverbial Wonga-Wonga bird, I went round in ever decreasing circles in streets that were virtually empty. To my relief, I came across an intelligent looking chap, stopped the car and sought directions. He turned out to be a Greek on holiday who spoke little English, but eventually I met a native who helped me on my way. Geoffrey Smith, Dr Stefan Buczacki and Daphne Ledward also met Ken Ford's exacting broadcasting standards and for some years we and the 'old boys' served as a varied team. Finally, Fred became terminally ill, Alan and Bill retired, and the new team took over under Ken's chairmanship. Little did we know then that Ken's days were numbered. The first inkling I had that all was not well was at the International Garden Festival in June 1984, where we were recording a programme. Stefan and Geoffrey had gone somewhere and Ken and I were alone backstage when he told me that he was suffering recurring chest pains. I advised him to see his doctor, who diagnosed cancer, and within a few months Ken had left us for the promised land. A little later, Ken's assistant and the members of the team paid me the compliment of asking me to chair the programme and with the concurrence of Michael Green, our master at BBC Manchester, I stepped into the shoes of my eminent pre-decessors.

I knew that Ken was a hard act to follow, but again I was fortunate. The team backed me to the hilt and Diana Stenson, our new producer, was a tower of strength. I was fully aware that my responsibilities were many and heavy. I had accepted the chairmanship of Radio 4's most popular programme and I had to maintain the devotion and respect it had engendered from its many thousand listeners since it first went on the air in 1947.

'GQT' now has a team of four to draw on, since Daphne and Stefan were joined by Fred Downham and Sue Phillips. Stefan and Fred are regular panellists, and our two girls alternate appearances depending on availability and location. At the risk of boosting their egos beyond the point of no return, I must confess that they are almost irreplaceable – not quite, but almost! To qualify as a 'GQT' panellist calls for a rare combination of talents and attributes. He or she must have a voice and a microphone manner acceptable to the listening public, and must also possess the inborn ability to work in a team, on and off mike. Such people are as rare as apples on pear trees! My role as chairman of that lot is more catalytic than anything else, although my own gardening know-how and experience comes in useful on occasion. My functions on stage are twofold. In the first place, I must put our audience at ease and keep them attentive, interested and amused throughout the recording, which is not all that difficult. We often visit societies and clubs that have waited up to twenty years for us to materialise, and when we do they are so surprised and grateful that they hang on every word. I shall never forget the evening we turned up to record a programme with a society in a village somewhere in England. They had waited sixteen years and we were welcomed with open arms. We sat down to a good pre-programme meal with members of the committee and then withdrew to a backstage room to prepare for the big event. Ken Ford was our chairman and the team was Bill, Geoffrey and myself. Ken was about to go on stage to begin proceedings when the society secretary entered and asked him to delay the start for a few minutes as his uncle in the audience had just died. Ken asked what was happening and was told that the old chap, complete with chair, had been taken outside the hall. I pointed out that it was raining and the reply was, 'Well, he won't notice it, will he?' Ken's offer to cancel the recording was met with the realistic response – 'We've waited sixteen years for you to come and nothing is going to stop us now!' – of such stuff are gardeners made!

My second function on stage is to exercise a modicum of

control over the team. One or two members tend to 'go on a bit' at times and, in fairness to the others and to the audience, their verbosity must be curtailed. On rare occasions there are slips of the tongue, technical errors caused, not by lack of knowledge but by fleeting lapses of concentration. My right ear is attuned to them, while in my left ear a custom-made earpiece is in verbal communication with our producer in the recording van outside the venue. During the recording Diana may issue instructions, or ply me with questions which I can answer only by using prearranged hand signals aimed at a camera at the back of the hall. My mute replies on a television screen in the van are as comprehensible as the spoken word. Ah, the marvels of twentieth-century science!

Our audiences and venues can vary enormously. We record programmes in village halls, schools, hotels, clubs and guild-halls, to name a few. In numbers, our audiences range from about a hundred people packed into a village hall not much bigger than a garden shed, to a guildhall where I remember an audience of over a thousand gardeners and friends. It was at this venue that the late Professor Alan Gemell made his classic *faux pas*. In reply to a questioner, what he intended to say was, 'I don't want to be circumspect', but everyone in the hall heard him say 'I don't want to be circumcised.' There was a momentary deathly hush until, unable to control myself, I exploded with mirth and over a thousand people joined in. One unforgettable venue was the Sid Pudsey Pavilion some-where in the Midlands. The large room had a long bar at the far end and during the recording members of our all-male audience made numerous trips to the pumps to replenish their glasses, and almost as many trips to the gents to maintain a liquid equilibrium. To add to our suffering, it was mid-winter and the building was devoid of heating. It says much for the team that we recorded an excellent programme under trying circumstances.

We experienced further toilet trauma in Leominster. Our correspondence editions are recorded in the afternoon, at the venue where we record an audience programme in the evening. On this particular occasion our venue was an hotel, where a large ballroom had been booked for the evening event. Unfortunately, it had been previously reserved by a local organisation in the afternoon, so we were allocated a large bedroom on the first floor complete with a four-poster bed, for our 'letters' programme. All went well until someone in the bedroom immediately above us went to the lavatory and pulled the chain. The sound effect was comparable to the Niagara Falls in flood and we stopped recording until the water cistern had refilled and silence was restored. We pressed on, but within minutes the cacophony of sound was repeated and repeated and repeated. We had a problem, as indeed had the occupant of the room above! We considered asking him, or her to 'ablute' elsewhere, but our sympathy overrode our frustration! Our other recording hazards include overhead aircraft, passing trains, road traffic, rattling windows and tin roofs, among other extraneous noises. Tin roofs are no problem unless it starts raining heavily during the recording, when the peace is shattered by a rising crescendo of sound. We stop, try to keep our audience amused with anecdotes and pray for better weather. However, our strangest venue was a mental institution. Ken Ford had accepted an invitation from the staff, but during the recording a number of inmates wandered in and, although they were well-behaved, it was very disconcerting. One chap ambled in dressed in pyjamas, raincoat and flat cap and sat in a seat directly in front of me. He didn't make a sound, but every time I answered a question his nods and facial expressions spoke volumes. I couldn't take my eyes off him.

Recording 'Gardeners' Question Time' takes us to all corners of the United Kingdom and beyond. We pay periodic visits to Northern Ireland and the Isle of Man and we have also accepted invitations from the British residents in Brussels and Paris. Wherever we are, we stay at good hotels where comfort, warmth and appetising food are assured, but it was not always so. In Ken Ford's day, some of the digs were decidedly non-star. I once had a basement, windowless room lit by a bare bulb, and my head hit a sloping ceiling when I sat up in bed. There was no bath, or shower and the toilet and wash-basin were in a room so narrow, that I was forced to wash and shave with my rear end in the bedroom! In another sub-standard establishment the cooking was so bad, that we walked to a nearby Little Chef for breakfast.

Stefan is particularly demanding of his creature comforts. I have arrived at our appointed accommodation on numerous occasions to meet him coming out, dark-browed and muttering, 'I'm not stopping here.' We move on and find a better place to lay our weary heads. Good hotels are essential to our morale and well-being. When we have an audience we put on a two-hour show and answer about sixteen to eighteen questions, many of them 'off the floor' and unrehearsed. When the recording is over, I feel as limp as a day-old lettuce and we all beat a path to our hotel, to enjoy rejuvenating beverages and a snack meal. We relax and wallow in the friendship of each other's company before toddling off to bed. It is decreed that we meet for breakfast at 8.30 a.m. sharp, and the team's choice of dishes is, I believe, revealing: Stefan has kippers, but only if they still possess their heads and tails. Fred will eat anything except eggs, which have revolted him ever since he once ate over twenty hard-boiled eggs at one sitting, because there was nothing else. Diana has a full breakfast, preceded by a mixed bowlful of prunes and All Bran – a moving experience! Sue is permanently on a diet and nibbles at grapefruit segments. Daphne is also slimming and, to strengthen her resolve, eats everything within sight. Sue Number Two, Diana's assistant, has scrambled eggs, and I tuck into a plateful of cold ham, top-dressed with a little English mustard. Thus fortified, we are ready to face another day. The team tackles individual mounds of correspondence, while Diana and I do a critical analysis of the previous evening's recording, and decide which questions to use and which to discard. Then I sift through piles of questions sent in by the societies or clubs that are our next ports of call, and select the twelve we will use. Finally, I go through a heap of our listeners' cards and letters and choose a number that are 'possibles' for a future correspondence edition. That all done, we pay our bills, load our luggage and either head for home, or onward to our next venue to record more programmes. It's a great life and we actually get paid (not a lot) for what we thoroughly enjoy doing.

I used to wonder how a radio programme on gardening had managed to retain its popularity and high listening audience for coming up to half a century. I know that we have listeners who have no garden and have never put seed to soil, because I have met them. So what is the programme's universal appeal? The answer came from two listeners. The first was a lady who, with her husband and young family, said quite simply, 'When I hear your voice I know everything's all right.' The second was a consultant surgeon who approached me at a garden centre and conveyed his thanks to the team and I for 'the only half hour of sanity on the radio'. From their remarks, it is apparent that in addition to offering sound advice on gardening problems the programme's down to earth character is a reassurance in a world shadowed by conflict, cruelty and unrest.

Towards the 1980s the strain of being involved in both radio and television programmes was beginning to tell. In my car I covered about 36,000 miles a year and often I had to dash from one programme to the other. Naturally, Glen resented my long and repeated absences and was worried that I was pushing my physical endurance to the limit. I had to make a choice and by mutual consent, I left the highly competitive time-consuming sphere of television, to devote more time and energy to my first love, radio.

At least that was my intention, but I succumbed to temptation. On the first occasion I was approached by an independent television company, Antelope West, based in Bristol. One of their number had conceived the idea of filming a series of twenty nature programmes depicting the everyday life of the flora and fauna inhabiting a hundred acres of British countryside. The area in question on the Welsh/English border was a mere thirty minutes' drive from home and it was basically unspoilt compared with the desecration that has been inflicted on much of our countryside. I was taken to walk the area and became enchanted with it on sight. Sheep and cows grazed the meadows and creatures of the wild roamed free. In one of the fields a large pond was home to moorhens and became a jellied mass of frog spawn followed by a population explosion of tadpoles. Predators thinned their numbers and in due course those that matured into frogs swam and leapt under a wide cover of water crowfoot in full bloom. On the wooded hillsides dwelt foxes and badgers, and our gifted cameraman captured their magical movements on film. A vixen gave birth to eight cubs and we followed their playful progress. In May the woodland floor erupted under a carpet of bluebells, the hedgerows were alive with wild flowers and later we gorged ourselves on blackberries. Above us, buzzards performed their aerobatics and on the valley floor fish and damselflies disturbed the placid waters of the Usk. A pair of swans made their nest in a riverside pool, ignored our unobtrusive presence and reared a family of six cygnets. We filmed a mink catching an eel and taking it home to feed its young, and on one sun-blessed morning as I sat on the riverbank the swans swam by in Indian file, led by proud dignified father with mother fussing at the rear of the column.

My involvement with the 'Hundred Acres' programme brought me nearer to the animals and plant that share our world than ever before and I learnt a lot about their private lives, which few people are privileged to see. Much of it was due to the expertise and dedication of Martin Dhorn our cameraman. He would often be in his hide before dawn to capture the slow awakening of life in the steamy silence of a summer morn. His moving pictures were edited in the Bristol studio and most of my time was spent in an airless cubby-hole, putting a voice to Martin's genius from a prepared script. It usually took most of a morning to dub the fifteen minute programme in English. In the afternoon the whole thing was repeated with a commentary in Welsh, my native tongue. The end products were viewed on Channel 4 in English and in Welsh on S4C, and they proved very popular with a public that seldom ventures into Nature's secret domain.

My second submission to television was to do with Garden Festival Wales, at Ebbw Vale. The BBC transmitted a daily programme called 'Summer Scene' from the festival and I was asked to contribute a weekly gardening slot. As chairman of the Wales In Bloom Foundation I had been involved with the festival and the Borough of Blaenan Gwent from the very beginning, so it seemed only natural that I should further the interests of the event and its locality. The two million visitors who came to Ebbw Vale saw a lovely landscape of gardens, massed bedding, huge man-made lakes and a towering water-fall amid a host of fun and entertainment for all the family. What they didn't see, or could even imagine, was the festival site as it once was – an area of grey-black dirt and the dross of steel production. When Richard Llewelyn wrote *How Green Was My Valley* he may well have stood on the mountain over-looking Ebbw Vale and looked down on a scene that typified Man's disregard for Nature's beauty in his quest for pro-duction and profit.

Now the scars have gone and the people of Ebbw Vale are pleased, not least of all Mrs Mary Evans. Born and bred in the town, she has lived in a terraced house overlooking the festival site ever since she married many years ago. For the first 'Summer Scene' programme I suggested that I should dem-onstrate planting a hanging basket. Our producer agreed, and further suggested that I should interview Mary and ask her why the front of her house was not adorned with flowers in keeping with the vista below. Her reply was a combination of heartbreak and hope. In the early days of her wedded life she had tried, but as she put it, 'the flowers turned black and died'. So vile and obnoxious were the emissions from the blast furnaces that it is a wonder anything or anyone lived in the polluted air. Thank God, the valley is green again.

There is one other television appearance that I shall always remember. It was the one and only time that I have been totally nonplussed in front of a camera. As an ex-serviceman I was invited as a guest to participate in a BBC Wales television programme on Remembrance Sunday. A week prior to the day, the producer called to establish my background, etc., and asked whether I had any photographs of myself in uniform. Glen dug deep into our archives and produced a heap of photographs, including one of my orderly Hynes and I, taken in the Shan States. The producer was intrigued and asked who my companion was. I told him all I knew and mentioned that in 1946 the Hynes family lived in Swansea. He asked if he could borrow the photograph and then, along with his copious notes, he departed. On Remembrance Sunday I was seated in the studio on a settee and, when the time came, Roy Noble the interviewer began plying me with questions. We chatted for a while and then on the monitor screen came the photograph of Hynes and I. Roy asked who the other fellow was, I told him and simultaneously a voice from behind the scenes said, 'How about a game of crib?' and there appeared ex-Private Gordon Hynes, whom I hadn't set eyes on for over forty years. I was lost for words – all I could say was, 'Good God, hello.'

Our move to the Welsh-English border country near the Severn estuary in 1979 demanded still more of my time at home. Here, in the mild, salt-laden air, I had found growing conditions that were very different from the windswept slopes of North Wales. For the first time in my life I had deep, fertile soil, sheltered from wind, and the sun shone from dawn to late afternoon in spring and summer. Nothing and nowhere is perfect and our new home had many faults. In the first place, the cottage had been neglected for decades. A succession of owners had come and gone, seldom settling in the place for longer than two years or so. It had even served time as a hippy commune and in their wake the inhabitants left vast areas of large-leaved comfrey and butterbur. It has taken me years to be rid of them. I've been told by a neighbour that in the 1950s the cottage was almost derelict and was bought by a local farmer who used it to house his calves. Our immediate pre-decessors were freelancers who dabbled in all kinds of things, including breeding Siamese cats and Afghan hounds. The dogs had been housed in a large wire-netting enclosure, surfaced with two tons of road chippings, in the very spot where I planned to grow vegetables. I cursed these chippings at first, but they came in useful to infill ground that had been over-excavated when someone had put up an 18 feet by 10 feet greenhouse – the garden's only asset. I still find it strange that in an acre of ground, adjoining a centuries-old cottage, the only ornamental plant was a flourishing Mock Orange. Even derelict cottages have their daffodils, a clump of rhubarb and an overgrown gooseberry bush, but here there was nothing except comfrey, butterbur and a rampant population of prize-winning weeds.

We knew when we bought it that the cottage was in need of attention. It had been built long before damp-courses were thought of and the rear walls were decidedly moist at the base. To make matters worse, the ground at the back of the house rose steeply a mere three feet away from the walls and was mostly sandstone rock. Heavy machinery was needed to rip it apart. A man with a JCB arrived and scooped out tons of earth and rock, leaving space for a large patio. To save the expense of carting the dross away, it was dumped up on a part of the bank, completely covering a large area to a depth of several feet in some places. When it was done the bank resembled a lunar landscape and our neighbours were aghast at our apparent wanton destruction of the environment. I wasn't worried. I knew that nature abhors barren soil and would redress the balance. Within weeks the exposed stones were clothed with moss and in between them the natural flora sprang to life, as if nothing had happened.

We laid the patio and then I tackled the job of building a dry-stone retaining wall around it, with the plentiful supply of stones that had been gouged out by the JCB. In places, the wall needed to be 8 feet high, sloping to a height of about 4 feet on either side. It was not easy and I made the mistake of rushing the job. Sandstone rocks are ungrained and will not split, they just shatter under a sledgehammer. The wall went up and within a year the high middle section collapsed in a messy heap on the patio. A single large rock at the base slipped and brought the whole lot down with it. Building a dry-stone wall with odd-shaped rocks is bad enough, rebuilding a fallen section is worse still. I'd learnt my lesson, and took my time rebuilding it. Ten years on, the wall is firm and stout, weatherworn and draped with plants. I planted a *Cotoneaster dammeri* at the top and what was a small container-grown plant now cascades its branches right down to the patio floor and has meandered sideways to a span of fifteen feet. Its small glossy leaves are ever present and the tiny white summer flowers are alive with bees. In winter the green-clad wall is beaded with red berries that bring a warm look to ice-cold days. In summer the pink flowers of soapwort – *Saponaria ocymoides* pour over the stones and vie with the bright-blue bells of campanulas for our attention. The wall and its plants look as though they were planted when the cottage was built, so well-established and homely do they seem.

We had made our move in September, the very best time of year from a gardener's point of view. I had the winter months ahead to clear the ground and begin planting trees and shrubs on the grassy banks that slope gently up from the lower ground. I had brought nothing from North Wales except for a few pot plants, preferring to leave everything for our successors to enjoy. The trees, shrubs and perennials I'd planted there were well settled. The garden was their home and I felt that it would be an unwarranted liberty to uproot them. When I'm up in North Wales, I call on them and, by the look of them, they are grateful that I let them get on with their lives without disruption. The last time I saw it, the Lawson cypress was nearly as tall as the house and the Virginia creeper I planted now crosses the whole of the gable end, clothing the pebble-dashed wall in summer green and with fiery-red finery in autumn.

I'm often asked if our garden is open to the public and the answer is an emphatic no. For one thing, it isn't good enough in my opinion and, for another, we were discouraged from public exposure by our experiences in our previous garden in North Wales. It had appeared several times on television and its location became known, with disturbing results. There was the time a minibus drew up in the lane as we were having tea. It disgorged fourteen people who entered and walked round the garden without so much as a by your leave. Then again, at 6.45 one morning there was a knock on the door. I opened it in my dressing-gown and there stood a chap clutching a diseased potato plant. He wanted to know what to do with it. I could have told him! Instead I told him to go home and spray his crop with Bordeaux Mixture and off he went. When we moved, we swore that we would find a secret place away from the camera and prying eyes and we found it. No one can find us here and the local people respect our privacy.

Here we are and here we stay, among the friendliest of countryfolk, in a lovely part of the country between the placid Wye and the treacherous Severn. The pace of life is slow and relaxed and everyone has time to look at the morning. We are back in the heart of the countryside where we belong and once again we are at one with the wild. The trees around us are a-coo with woodpigeons. A pair of over-sexed starlings raise family after raucous family in the roof, and a couple of cheeky bluetits have made their home in a hole in the wall of our study. Down the lane I follow a very pregnant badger, so heavy with badgerettes, that I have to slow down to her lumbering pace until she turns off into a field. A hawk swoops and claws a terrified blackbird from the hedge. I round a corner and terrorise a female pheasant with a brood of tiny chicks. She panics and takes off over the hedge and into the field. The chicks go frantic and run in all directions. I try to count them. There must be a dozen at least and I start to shepherd them in the direction of the field gate. Mother, meantime, curses me and calls her chicks but, eventually, they are all in the field, or are they? No there's one idiot who is either deaf, blind, or both, and is hell-bent on reaching the busy A48 and certain death. I belt after it and, after much toing and froing, manage to catch the wayward infant and return it to its family. Father pheasant is resident in and around our garden. We've christened the blue-necked, brown-bodied bird Fred, and every day he takes a leisurely, stately walk all round, emitting a loud honk if one of our cats comes too close. I wish he would take more responsibility for his family. Bushy-tailed grey squirrels abound and foxes are a common sight, but they never trouble us. Chrys, the big tortoiseshell cat, once came face to face with a fox in the paddock across the lane and, placid creature that he is, took the only possible course of action – he sat down and stared at it. The two animals maintained immovable eye contact for several minutes and it was the fox that gave way and made off with his brush between his legs.

When we came here the place was alive with mice, but our six cats with four more of our neighbours' felines have reduced their population almost to extinction. I'm afraid that the cats do occasionally catch an unwary bird, but luckily they usually bring them home alive and Glen rescues most of them. They, like many animals in a similar situation, are resigned to death and it takes all her persuasive powers to convince them that there is still life to be lived. She cups the tiny creatures in her hands, talks to them in Welsh (although they are probably English-speaking) and blows gently into their nostrils. They stir, perk up and fly off – well, who wouldn't after a kiss of life like that! Cass, who has long since departed this earth, was adept at catching butterflies and moths which he ate with obvious relish, and more than once he actually caught and brought us a bat. How he managed to capture such a fast moving flyer is beyond us. But the most astonishing catch by one of our cats was a stoat – a vicious animal when threatened. We still don't know which one accomplished the feat, but I became aware that something was afoot when I entered my study. Aly was sitting there looking worried. Slight scuffling sounds came from behind a radiator, and the room smelt like a disused brewery. I climbed on a chair, peered behind the radiator and a pair of malevolent eyes stared back at me. I removed Aly, opened the outside door, got a bamboo cane and poked it at the stout, who fought it tooth and nail until it fell to the floor, and then scuttled behind the stairs. I gave up, left the door open and at some time the stoat left, taking its pervasive pong with it. Contrary to the conviction of people who visit, but do not live in the countryside, there is never a dull moment. From my window I look out on an everchanging scene. Every season brings its own beauty, every day it changes, and anticipation subdues boredom and depression.

I can cast an eye over my shoulder and look back on a life that has been incredibly kind. I grew up in the security of a loving family and a caring community, in which the quality of life was paramount. We found pleasure and peace in Nature's ambience. The pursuit of wealth and possession was not our ruling passion and there was time and space for self-expression. Best of all I have found a perfect partner and, as one, we have shared our joys and sorrows along life's way. Our two children have blessed us with five grandchildren who love us and in whose eyes we can do no wrong. What more can a man ask?

A Changing World

꿇

GARDENING, as we know it, is very different to the art our forebears practised, but we owe much of our modern expertise and our population of garden plants to others. The Roman invaders introduced not only plants new to Britain, but also new concepts. They built walls around their permanent encampments, and on them they grew and trained fruits and other plants. In due course, affluent society emulated the invaders, and wall-gardening became the vogue. The Greeks were the first to provide open parkland in or near centres of population where the 'townies' could escape from 'bricks and mortar', and spend their leisure time in more convivial surroundings. We got the message, and now every town and city boasts a public park where the locals can stroll, picnic, make love and feast their eyes on great beds of vibrant colour. To the Japanese we owe the concept of garden design, although too few gardeners are imaginative enough to depart from the suburban tradition of a rectangular plot with serried ranks of annual flowers bordering an equally rectangular area of grass that poses for a lawn.

To a handful of intrepid explorers, botanists, gardeners and their sponsors we give humble thanks for locating new plants in far-off lands and bringing them back to Britain. They often risked life and limb in pursuit of the almost unattainable, and it is fitting that their names are forever etched in gardening. The eighteenth and nineteenth centuries saw plant hunters beating a path to the Far East. At the turn of the century Ernest Wilson ventured into the very heartland of China and there he found the Handkerchief tree, *Davidia involucrata*, a magnolia new to Britain, the paperbark maple and, in all, a total of over three hundred plants. He discovered *Lilium regale* growing on the borders of Tibet, and visited China so often that he is known to this day as Chinese Wilson. *Berberis wilsoniae*, which he brought back in 1904, is his memorial, among many other plants. Robert Fortune gave us *Rhododendron fortunei*, George Forrest found *Pieris forrestii*, and to them and others we are eternally grateful.

By the mid-nineteenth century the winds of change became a gale that changed the face of horticulture. Until then, gardeners and farmers had been content in the knowledge that plants grew. They sought not the reason why, or how. They fed them with manure in plenty and were satisfied with the end result. Then in 1836 a certain Jules Von Liebig startled all sons of the soil. His research revealed that plants feed on chemicals contained in all manures, namely nitrogen, phosphorus and potassium. He expounded the NPK theory to all people, and rightly maintained that plants would grow by the application of the three elements in concentrated, inorganic form. It was the birth of the massive, multinational, multimillion-pound artificial fertiliser industry.

Natural manures contain less than half a per cent of these three essential plant foods. Therefore gardeners leapt with joy at the prospect of obtaining their fertilisers in handy, carry-home packs, rather than spending time and energy wheeling barrowloads of sweet-smelling 'muck' on to their plots and borders. Much as we owe to Von Liebig, his theory and its practise opened a perilous phase in agriculture and horticulture. We now know that repeated and excessive applications of artificial fertilisers pollute our rivers, but worse still was, and is, the degradation of the soil in the absence of natural manures. Von Liebig and others failed to appreciate that fertile soil is a living entity, composed of minerals and a mass of micro-organisms, existing in a symbiotic association with plants to their mutual benefit. To survive and prosper the organisms need a soil amply supplied with decayed organic matter in the form of manure or compost. Most gardeners are now aware of the necessity to maintain the soil's natural structure and balance. Twenty to thirty years ago there were very few compost bins in our gardens, today most gardeners have one as proof that it is never too late to mend our ways.

Compost of another kind has been the deep concern of several of my colleagues and I for some years. When I began gardening under Mother's supervision in the thirties, seed- and potting-composts were unheard of. We sowed seeds in shallow boxes of sieved garden soil which, as always, contained dormant weed seeds. In the warmth of the kitchen window-sill they all germinated *en masse* and, unless one knew the difference between a marigold and a groundsel seedling, it was all a waste of effort. The trick I learnt was to sow the selected seeds in straight rows. The seedlings emerged in regimented ranks and thus were easily distinguishable from the weeds.

In the mid 1930s the John Innes Horticultural Institute made a sensational advance that has been of tremendous benefit to both professional and amateur gardeners. The boffins invented seed- and potting-composts that were weed-free, and contained a balanced plant food. They consisted of measured quantities of sterilised loam, peat, sand and organic fertiliser, formulated to give seedlings and more mature plants an ideal diet, free from weed competition. These composts are still available, but they have been largely superseded by the soilless formulations that flooded the market, and revolutionised seed sowing, some time in the 1960s. These were greeted with a fanfare of trumpets. They were lighter in weight, cleaner, easier to use and supported excellent growth. They were composed of balanced fertilisers mixed into sphagnum peat and nothing else. I used them by the big bagfuls for twenty years or more – everyone did, without a thought that they might be environmentally harmful. It never occurred to me to question the source of peat supply, until I was told. Peat is a natural resource in the wetland bogs of Britain and elsewhere. It is the direct result of centuries of plant decomposition and it supports its own specialised flora and fauna that cannot adapt to any other environment. Peat bogs will not regenerate and their removal has left a landscape that is so changed and destroyed as to be virtually inert. An alternative to peat had to be found before avaricious industry completely destroyed vast tracts of precious, irreplaceable wetland. We now have that alternative, and anyone using peat in any shape or form from now on deserves to be deposited at the bottom of a runner bean trench, and heavily mulched with pig manure! I bet the beans would crop well!

At present, the best peat alternative is a byproduct of the coconut industry, called coir. It is natural waste material, and there are mountains of the stuff in countries such as Sri Lanka. It is shipped to our shores, mixed with plant foods and sold as Coir Multipurpose Compost. Hopefully, it will save much of what remains of our peat bogs, and it contributes to the economy of lands that could use a helping hand. Other peat alternatives derived from organic waste, are also coming on the market. I welcome a mulch material made from cocoashell, a cast-off from cocoa-bean production. Like shredded bark, it is great stuff to add as a mulch around trees, shrubs, roses and other plants, to smother weed growth and conserve soil moisture at a time when the threat of global warming is very real.

Herbicides and pesticides are now household words used by every gardener who values his plants. Fifty years ago I didn't use any. To begin with there were few available, and also there didn't seem to be as many pests around. There were fewer people, fewer gardens and as a result cultivation was less intense. Nevertheless, pests there were and we had ways of coping with them. We sprayed our roses with a viscous concoction made from boiled rhubarb sticks and leaves, and most of the time it worked. Slugs and snails were kept at bay by sprinkling crushed eggshells, sharp sand, or gorse needles around susceptible plants. We also made a lethal slugicide by mixing powdered 'meta' with bran, or brown flour. There were other ways of killing slugs. Many years ago an advertisement appeared in the papers offering 'certain death to slugs'. Readers were invited to send 2/6d (12½ pence) and in return they would receive the magic slugicide. Hundreds did, and through the post came two blocks of wood, one marked A and the other marked B. The instructions read as follows: 'Place slug on block A and belt it with block B.' A crafty con, but I suspect that more gardeners chuckled than complained.

From the 1950s until fairly recently pesticides flooded the market. Gardeners used them with gay abandon, with no thought that they could be harmful to humans as well as pests. It took several years and much lobbying of governments to convince the powers that be and manufacturers that certain chemical pesticides were possible health hazards. The widespread use and sale of DDT and the aldrin group of chemicals were banned in Britain, although I believe they are still used abroad in countries where controls are lax, and profitable production outweighs human life. For this reason, among others, I prefer to grow my own fruit and vegetables, safe in the knowledge that they are fresh and untainted. Modern pesticides fall into two categories: one kills on contact and the other kills by entering the plants' sap system and destroying the predators that feed on plant tissue. As far as is known, they are people-safe, although I do not use the systemic pesticides on edible crops. I prefer to take no chances.

Herbicides are, arguably the greatest of all modern developments in gardening and farming. Weeds in lawns are, and always will be, a problem. I remember spending long hours on my hands and knees, digging out perennial weeds by hand. It was soul-destroying. Nowadays, selective lawn herbicides kill flat-leaved weeds such as docks, dandelions and daisies, leaving the grass unharmed. They contain hormones which are absorbed by the leaves, and cause the plants to grow at an abnormally rapid rate, outstripping their ability to sustain their mad burst of growth, and they collapse. The grasses are practically unaffected, because the herbicide drips off their narrow leaves.

Two of the most persistent weeds in the garden are con-

volvulus and ground elder. Years ago their complete eradi-
cation was virtually impossible. Both weeds have long,
ramifying root systems and any attempt at digging them out
was only partly successful. The tiniest piece of root left in the
ground gave birth to new plants and a new population of
weeds sprang to life with renewed vigour. The only herbicide
available to gardeners was sodium chlorate. It killed the weeds
all right, but it also annihilated everything else in its path and
left the soil toxic and unplantable for up to three years! We
bought it as crystals which we were advised to dissolve in
tepid water, but it was also applied in solid form on paths and
drives, with dire results on more than one occasion. Sodium
chlorate has three oxygen atoms, one of which is unstable and
prone to spontaneous ignition under certain conditions, as an
unfortunate lady once discovered. It was a hot summer's day
when she applied the chlorate to her drive. The heat and
possibly a spark ignited the chemical, and the poor lady was
engulfed in a fatal sheet of flame.

I well remember the first inkling I had of the existence of a
new, revolutionary herbicide. I had been recording a television
programme with my old friend, the late, lamented Percy
Thrower. After the recording he took me to his newly-built
house near Shrewsbury. We drove in through the gates and I
noticed that the rough grass on each side of the drive was
brown and dead. I assumed an application of sodium chlorate
had been used, until I saw that squares of turf had been
removed and in their place grew Brussels sprouts – how come?
With a glint in his eye, Percy explained. He was testing a
new herbicide called paraquat, soon to be marketed under the
brand name Weedol. It kills all top growth, yet loses its toxicity
in the soil very quickly. Although deep-rooted perennial weeds
like dandelions will regrow, all annual weeds such as groundsel and chickweed are done to death. This was great news for
gardeners, and there was even more rejoicing some years later
when the herbicide glyphosate hit the headlines. At last we had
a systemic herbicide that penetrated right down to a weed's
deepest roots, killing it once and for all. Nothing could go

wrong, could it? Oh, yes, it could! I still get letters from gardeners who believe that anything labelled weedkillers only kills weeds. There was the chap who painstakingly watered his lawn with glyphosate to kill daisies and ended up with a quarter of an acre of dead grass three weeks later. The moral is: read the instructions on the pack, then you can't go wrong. Used properly and in the correct amounts, herbicides and pesticides are the gardeners' friends; used incorrectly, they can do irreparable damage and may even kill the user.

Nowadays, life without garden centres seems inconceivable, yet their appearance on the gardening scene can be measured in less than half a lifetime. Before they began to exert their massive influence on the retail market, gardeners bought almost all their needs by mail-order. We purchased our trees, roses, shrubs, herbaceous plants, seeds and even fertilisers from catalogues, and there were limitations. Trees, shrubs and roses were delivered as bare-root plants, which meant that all deciduous subjects could be lifted and despatched only during their dormant period between November and March at the latest. Garden centres have extended the buying and planting season to encompass the whole year. Trees and shrubs are now container-grown and a novice gardener may select a rose bush, for instance, in full bloom and plant it with every chance of success. Furthermore, the plants bear labels listing the plants' characteristics and attributes. Nevertheless, purchasing errors are not uncommon. As one strolls between the rows of potted beauties, there is an irresistible urge to put a pretty little thing in the trolley and take it home. It is planted near a window where it can be seen and admired, and before you can say 'Aspidistra', the pretty little thing is ten feet tall and your sitting-room is in permanent darkness. Without doubt, garden centres have contributed largely to the increase in the knowledge and practice of gardening over the past two decades.

Mechanisation is yet another factor that has prompted more gardening. Push and shove mowers are in the minority, having given way to petrol and electricity-powered models. There are powered hedge clippers and soil cultivators, although I hold that there is nothing to beat digging by hand. Contrary to popular belief I find digging relaxing and rewarding, when it is done at a leisurely pace. My mind meanders to pleasant thoughts and memories. I commune with Nature, and the robin that waits to steal a worm becomes a trusting friend. There are garden shredders that reduce twigs and prunings to a valuable, usable mulch material at little cost, and chainsaws for cutting through branches and fell trees. They have all taken much of the toil, sweat and tears out of gardening, but a price has to be paid for convenience. Weekends were once peaceful; now the air is rent with the roar of petrol engines, the undulating, ear-splitting whine of chainsaws and the strangulated sound of shredders masticating wood. I almost wish I lived in Germany, where the use of such mechanical contrivances is banned at weekends and even car-washing is *verboten*. But somehow I couldn't come to terms with a country where a motorway exit road is called an *Ausfahrt*!

Greenhouses have followed the advances made in gardening technology and their popularity has increased by hundreds. Once they were built on site, of wood and glass on brick walls and heated by coal-fired boilers that fed water through 4-inch pipes. I know because I spent hours declinkering and stoking them. Today's greenhouses are delivered in sections, and erected quickly by anyone other than me, who finds it impossible to follow the easy-to-follow instructions. Treated cedar-wood houses and aluminium structures are glass-to-ground, to admit maximum light and promote optimum growth. They can be equipped with automatic ventilators that open magically as the temperature rises and close as it drops. There are automatic watering systems but, as yet, no one has invented an automatic transplanting machine, thank heavens! Plants need and respond to the touch of human hands and a few tender words from a caring gardener. Thermostatically controlled, electric propagators ensure the successful germination of tender plant seeds at a cost of only a few pence a day. Temperature controlled fan-heaters will more than repel frost, and enable a gardener to enjoy spring in his greenhouse while it is still winter outside. The outcome of it all is that now there are more greenhouses in gardens than ever, and the range of plants grown in them is more extensive. It is not uncommon to find peppers, cucumbers, aubergines and other exotics growing alongside the ubiquitous tomato.

Gardening styles have also changed, to keep pace with modern living. For the most part, today's garden is a solitary place from Monday to Friday. The children attend school, and both parents are out earning their crusts from morn to eve. They have less time than their forebears to tend their gardens, and there are other calls upon their time at weekends. The shopping needs to be done, there are people to visit and games to be played. In their gardens these busy people have to equate time and space. They can't spare the time to raise lots of plants, weed their borders and undertake other time-consuming tasks. The plants they grow need to be reasonably self-sufficient and capable of suppressing weed growth. So, in place of beds of annual plants, they have, or should have, mixed borders of shrubs and herbaceous perennials, with a few spaces left to plant annuals and bulbs to vary the scene a little from season to season.

What of tomorrow's gardeners, of a generation as yet unborn? There is talk of genetic engineering. Not content with the natural way of things, the tireless boffins seem intent on fiddling around with plant cells in an endeavour to produce bigger and better (?) plants, higher yields, more colour, and earlier this and that. It frightens me. Look what happened to cattle. When I joined the gardening industry in 1952 bone meal fertiliser was cheap. Suddenly the price increased by leaps and bounds. I sought the reason and discovered that it was being incorporated into animal feed. Bone meal is derived from animal tissue and there we were, feeding it back to animals that are naturally herbivarous. We were advocates of a kind of cannibalism – little wonder that herds were afflicted with mad cow disease. Nature has maintained a balance of life for millions of years, and I am convinced that we invade her privacy and tinker with her laws at our own peril.

If we are to believe what we hear, we have created a hole in the ozone layer that from time immemorial has protected our planet from global warming. On the assumption that the hole does not get bigger and out of control, global warming could be to our advantage. We may see the day when the exotic plants of the subtropics are widely grown in British gardens that are never smitten by frost. In my imagination I see our cottage porch dressed overall with bougainvillea, avenues of frangipanis line our streets, oranges and lemons fruit in our orchards, and my great-grandchildren will learn how to harvest coconuts. I wonder?

My generation has much to answer for. 'We have followed too much the devices and desires of our own hearts' in our endless quest for the trivia of materialism. We pollute our air, our rivers and our soil. We destroy forests and habitats that have been the homes of plants and animals that are entitled to expect a peaceful co-existence with us. Fortunately, realisation is dawning, albeit slowly. There is a growing trend towards conservation and preservation in the face of wanton destruction. Most gardens have a compost-heap now, and organic gardening is no longer regarded as cultivation by cranks. There are even seed companies who supply wild flower seeds to attract and sustain wildlife in our gardens. We feed the birds whose habitats have been destroyed by intensive farming, and some of us leave a patch of nettles in our gardens, providing maternity units for Peacock, Tortoiseshell and other butterflies.

A lifetime spent in gardening has taught me many things. I am more aware that growth is finite. The life of an annual plant spans less than a year, whereas there are giants of the forest that grow and live for centuries, but even they meet their Maker in the fullness of time. It is a lesson that companies and governments should heed. The concept of endless growth dominates their policies and practices, but there must come a time when further growth, stemming from greed, can only spell disaster. Stability is surely better than surrender to insatiable demand.

I have also come to realise that plants are far more sophisticated and better adapted to life than people. They manufacture their own food, utilising the chlorophyll in their leaves to harness atmospheric carbon dioxide, and soil water to produce sugars and starches. We are primitive by comparison. We feed ourselves by inserting quantities of solids into holes in our heads, and what follows beggars description! Not only that, plants do not rely solely on sexual relationships to perpetuate their kind. We propagate plants from cuttings. Think about it. We sever a limb of a tree, insert the cut end into the soil, and, miraculously, it roots and grows into a mirror image of its parent. Now imagine the consequences if I severed half an arm, or a leg and inserted it into something that, for want of anything better, I'll call a suitable growing medium. The answer is obvious, my 'cutting' would rot and I would be minus an appendage.

For these and other reasons I have the greatest respect and admiration for the plants that share our planet. It is my fervent hope that future generations will do all in their power to preserve our heritage.